Nouvelle
Chinese
Cooking

BOOKS BY KAREN LEE WITH ALAXANDRA BRANYON

SOUP, SALAD AND PASTA INNOVATIONS
CHINESE COOKING SECRETS

BOOKS BY KAREN LEE

CHINESE COOKING FOR THE AMERICAN KITCHEN

Nouvelle Chinese Cooking

by KAREN LEE
Written with ALAXANDRA BRANYON

Macmillan Publishing Company • New York
Collier Macmillan Publishers • London

Macmillan Publishing Company
866 Third Avenue, New York, N.Y. 10022
Collier Macmillan Canada, Inc.

Library of Congress Cataloging-in-Publication Data
Lee, Karen.
  Nouvelle Chinese cooking.
  Includes index.
  1. Cookery, Chinese. 2. Cookery, French.
I. Branyon, Alaxandra. II. Title.
TX724.5.C5L455 1987   641.5951   87-18609
ISBN 0-02-570060-X

Macmillan books are available at special discounts for bulk purchases for sales promotions, premiums, fund-raising, or educational use. For details, contact:

Special Sales Director
Macmillan Publishing Company
866 Third Avenue
New York, N.Y. 10022

10 9 8 7 6 5 4 3 2 1

Printed in the United States of America
Designed by Beth Tondreau Design

To Lindley Boegehold

Contents

Acknowledgments

I would like to thank Alaxandra Branyon, my writing collaborator. She has gone beyond the call of duty with this book as she has done in the past by contributing endless hours of her expertise, time and involvement. She not only writes well about food, she truly understands it.

My supportive, patient, motivating, experimental class once again came through for me every Monday night to help test all the recipes again and again until they were perfect.

Joan Snyder Lewisohn has been as valuable a consultant on this book as she has been my longtime friend.

A special thanks to Colette Linnihan, who is a tremendous pillar of support in my life and who is helping me to realize my full potential.

Introduction

As I walked into Lindley Boegehold's office at Macmillan Publishing Company, she greeted me with, "So you want to do another book."

For the next hour and a half we talked about all kinds of different ideas, none of them really grabbing either one of us. We were about to call it a day when she said, "Don't you do anything nouvelle like Wolfgang Puck or any of those California chefs?"

My whole last book incorporated French cooking techniques into classic Chinese cuisine. The defatting, reducing, and deglazing of sauces, for instance, gives certain dishes such as Orange Spiced Duck an added refinement that is satisfying and appealing to the Western palate.

But that wasn't exactly what she meant. She had something more extreme in mind—a real blending of Eastern and Western ingredients and cooking techniques. She said, "I don't care if you stuff wontons with goat cheese."

"That's a great idea," I said, and left her office filled with excitement. Never before had an editor given me a premise for a whole book. Now for the first time I would be breaking new ground in a field to which I had devoted twenty years of my life.

In the past I developed recipes that were for the most part variations on Chinese classics. In recreating traditional dishes, I gave them a style of my own that went beyond the parroting of the recipes of the masters but I rarely created a dish from scratch.

Now I was free to experiment, with or without a traditional source of reference, limited only by my own imagination. I could pair French, American, Italian, Japanese, Indian, or any other cuisine's ingredients and techniques with Chinese. I could take a Western classic such as Italian white clam sauce and easternize it, an example of which is the shrimp and scallop dish called Linguini with Seafood Coriander Sauce. I could take a Chinese classic such as a Cantonese soong dish and westernize it, drastically altering it so as to render it inauthentic and deliciously original, as is the case of Soong Stuffed Loin of Veal. When my perspective changed, wontons no longer were filled with pork and shrimp. They became outrageously French with fresh goat cheese and rosemary, accented with a spike of Italian sun-dried tomatoes and olive paste.

Spring rolls got revolutionized with fresh Italian cremini, dried porcini, and fresh French chanterelles. With the advent of these Wild Mushroom Spring Rolls, I can't get my catering clients to order the traditional ones.

Sichuan Sauce, composed of fermented soybean-based sauces to which a homemade hot sauce is added, landed on sautéed whole veal chops, combining an American favorite entrée, a French cooking technique, and a popular Chinese seasoning sauce. Furthermore, this version of Sichuan Sauce is enriched with a dash of cream, white wine, and shallots.

Cream! The whole idea of introducing dairy products into Chinese cooking is unheard of. They don't have dairy products because there has always been a scarcity of cattle in China due to a lack of suitable grazing land. That's why pork, not beef, has been the featured meat, and why it's heresy to use cream or butter.

Instead of sautéing with butter the Chinese stir-fry over extremely high heat with peanut oil, which has a great resistance to becoming saturated. But I love the flavor butter gives, for instance, to certain sautéed vegetables; therefore I used it in such a dish as Tea Smoked Lobster with Lemon Caper Sauce to sauté the shallots and to enrich the sauce for this lobster that has been smoked over Lapsang Souchong tea leaves, brown sugar, and raw rice.

In Sautéed Chicken Breasts with Orange Sauce, I employed butter in my adaptation of a beurre manié, for it is an excellent thickening agent when kneaded with water chestnut powder. I did the same for Peking Turkey, which is a magnificent Thanksgiving dish featuring an American bird that has parchment-crisp skin due to the Chinese air-drying technique.

How on earth did a beurre manié end up in a Chinese dish? How did a zip of candied ginger find its way into a frozen lemon soufflé with fresh raspberry sauce? Since when does a bouillabaisse from Marseille include winter melon and black bean aioli? What are green peppercorns and reduced chicken stock doing in

Chinese dishes? From where did these foods, spices, techniques, and ideas come?

A lot of people ask me how I became a good cook.

My first exposure to real cooking was in Marseilles, France. I was sixteen years old and living with a French family. That summer in their villa overlooking the Mediterranean Sea I learned to speak French, how the French lived, and how they cooked. I absorbed on a daily basis the attitude of the people, whose deep appreciation of good food has been embedded in their culture for centuries.

Each day the freshest ingredients were bought at the market, and during every meal, the main focus was the food. I became aware of ingredients and cooking techniques, of how food tasted, and of the simplicity of flavors in their home-style French cooking, what is known as *la cuisine bourgeoise*.

This whole experience was the premise on which I founded my principles of cooking. I try to create the same atmosphere in my classes, where I teach students how to appreciate food in this tradition. When we eat the dinner we have prepared, the food is the main attraction for the evening.

In this Nouvelle Chinese approach, I blend characteristic elements of home-style and classic French cooking with Chinese and other cuisines. In doing so, I go beyond *la cuisine bourgeoise* but never forget its fundamentals.

Since time is of the essence for most American cooks (there seems to be a shortage of it), I have streamlined preparation procedures. In many cases you will see that I have eliminated the cutting and marinating of the meat. Cooking whole pieces of a tail of filet mignon or whole pieces of Norwegian salmon or sole fillet reduces the workload substantially.

Traditional Chinese cuisine gives the chef all the responsibility for the cutting and the seasoning of the entire meal. Cutting the food into bite-size pieces reduces the actual cooking time, thereby conserving on fuel. It also enables the diner to eat with chopsticks.

Cheap and plentiful labor to help with the preparation is not an option for the American cook. Therefore I thought, since we already have a set of flatware in the kitchen, why not let the eaters do some of the cutting, which they are accustomed to doing anyway.

So set the table with flatware *and* chopsticks. And take pleasure in knowing that these Nouvelle Chinese dishes can't be found on any restaurant menu—but are on your table between the silver and the bamboo.

Sauces

CHILI OIL

HOT SAUCE

CORIANDER DIPPING SAUCE

SPICY DIPPING SAUCE

SICHUAN PEPPERCORN POWDER

SPICY MUSTARD SAUCE

QUATRE FRUITS SAUCE

TOMATO SAUCE

Chili Oil

Since oil comprises 95 percent of the ingredients in the recipe, it is imperative that you use a good quality, such as Planters. When chili oil is properly made, it should smell like roasted hot peanuts.

1 cup peanut oil
⅓ cup crushed dried chili pepper

1. Place a 12-inch wok over high heat for about 1 minute or until it smokes. Pour in the oil. Turn the heat to medium and allow the oil to reach 350°. It is very important that the temperature of the oil be accurate. If the oil is too hot, the chili pepper will burn. If the oil is not hot enough, the Chili Oil will not take on the desired roasted aroma and wonderful flavor. Once the oil reaches 350°, remove the wok from the heat source and let stand 1 minute.

2. Add the crushed chili pepper to the wok all at once. Stir briefly with chopsticks. Allow the Chili Oil to cool in the wok, then place it in a covered glass jar and refrigerate. Stored in the refrigerator, Chili Oil will last at least 1 year.

Dried chili peppers, packaged in plastic bags, are sold in Oriental markets. They can be purchased crushed or whole. Because I prefer crushing them myself to bring out the flavor, I keep 2 coffee mills, one for grinding coffee and one for grinding spices.

Make a double batch of Chili Oil and strain half of it. Use the unstrained half for making Hot Sauce, which calls for the Chili Oil to be measured with the crushed chili pepper. Use the other half, in which the cooled Chili Oil has been strained and the crushed chili pepper has been discarded, for all other purposes.

YIELDS 1¼ cups

Hot Sauce

Hot Sauce, also called chili paste, is a major seasoning and the reason for the heat in Sichuan cooking. This very special hot sauce can be applied to many cuisines, such as in a Mexican chili, an Italian diavolo sauce, or an Indian curry. Students put it on open-faced melted cheese sandwiches, in a meat loaf, in vegetable soup—any time they want to make a dish spicy. At this point in my culinary career, I don't think I could cook without it.

¾ cup Chili Oil (see page 9)
¼ cup peanut oil
¼ cup minced garlic
1½ cups finely diced red sweet peppers
½ cup finely diced green bell peppers
2 teaspoons sugar
½ of a 7-ounce jar of roasted peppers
1 tablespoon red wine vinegar
1 tablespoon Oriental sesame oil

1. Make the chili oil and set aside ¾ cup, measured with the crushed chili.
2. Place a small wok over high heat for about 1 minute or until it smokes. Add the peanut oil. Turn the heat to low and heat for a few seconds. Add the garlic and sauté until it has lightly browned. Add the red sweet peppers and the green bell peppers. Turn the heat to high. Stir-fry about 2 minutes. Add the sugar and turn the heat to medium, continuing to cook another 8 to 10 minutes or until the peppers have softened and are thoroughly cooked. Turn off the heat.
3. Using the on-and-off technique, puree the roasted peppers with their juice in a food processor. Add them to the wok, along with the chili oil, vinegar, and sesame oil. Stir until well combined. Allow the sauce to cool; then place it in small glass jars with tight-fitting lids and refrigerate for up to 6 months.

Always stir the Hot Sauce before measuring, as the oil separates. One to 2 teaspoons will make a dish pleasantly spicy, but more or less can be added according to taste.

Stored in small lidded glass jars, Hot Sauce will keep for at least 6 months.

YIELDS approximately 1¾ cups

Coriander Dipping Sauce

Here's an alternative to soy-based dipping sauces. When you make a variety of appetizers, you may want to serve a number of dips, including Coriander Dipping Sauce, Spicy Mustard Sauce, Quatre Fruits Sauce, Spicy Dipping Sauce, and Sichuan Peppercorn Powder.

    2 tablespoons chopped coriander leaves
    ¼ cup Japanese rice vinegar
    2 teaspoons sugar
    1 tablespoon minced ginger
    1 teaspoon Hot Sauce (see page opposite)

    1. Combine the ingredients in a bowl.
    2. Coriander Dipping Sauce can be made early in the day and does not require refrigeration.

YIELDS ½ cup

Spicy Dipping Sauce

The great appeal of this dipping sauce may be attributed to the multiple layers of flavor, including its Japanese, French, Chinese, and Italian vinegars. Used traditionally for Chinese appetizers such as dim sum and butterfly shrimp, it is also good as an alternate selection on the crudité table. Blanch hard vegetables such as cauliflower and broccoli before serving.

¼ cup dark soy sauce
¼ cup light soy sauce
¼ cup Japanese rice vinegar
¼ cup red wine vinegar
¼ cup Chinese red vinegar
1 tablespoon balsamic vinegar
½ cup minced ginger
1 teaspoon Hot Sauce (see pp. 10–11)
1 teaspoon Oriental sesame oil
1 teaspoon sugar
1 teaspoon minced garlic
2 tablespoons finely chopped scallions, white and green parts included

1. Combine all the ingredients in a bowl.
2. Place the sauce in a lidded glass jar and refrigerate.

If you add the garlic and scallion on the day you serve it, Spicy Dipping Sauce can be stored in the refrigerator for 1 month.

Stir well before measuring the portion that you are going to use.

Depending on the amount of sauce required, add the appropriate amount of garlic and scallion.

YIELDS 2 CUPS

Sichuan Peppercorn Powder

These aromatic peppercorns are grown in Sichuan Province, a hot tropical inland area in the western part of China. Their flavor is intensified when they are dry-roasted in a wok, allowed to cool, and then pulverized in a coffee mill.

1 cup Sichuan peppercorns

1. Place a wok over high heat for about 1 minute or until it smokes. Add the peppercorns. Turn the heat to low. Dry-cook for 3 minutes, stirring slowly but constantly until the peppercorns turn darker brown. The peppercorns will start to smoke before they turn darker. Remove them from the wok. Let them cool.

2. Place the peppercorns in a coffee mill, food processor, or blender. Blend until they become a powder. Place the Sichuan Peppercorn Powder in a glass jar with a tight-fitting cover. Refrigerate the unused portion for up to 1 month.

These peppercorns will keep their aroma for 1 year if stored in a lidded glass jar on the shelf.

YIELDS 1 cup

Spicy Mustard Sauce

The mustard sauce offered in Chinese restaurants is composed of dry mustard and water. This concoction is far more flavorful, and can be used as a dip for hors d'oeuvres, to season salad dressings, in marinades, or on sandwiches.

One 2-ounce tin of Coleman's dry mustard
¾ cup medium-dry sherry
½ cup Dijon mustard
½ cup Pommery cracked seed mustard

1. Place the dry mustard in the bowl of a food processor.
2. Pulse the machine on and off while pouring the sherry through the feeding tube. Continue processing until you have a smooth, thick paste. Add more sherry if necessary.
3. Add the Dijon and the Pommery, then pulse on and off a few times. Adjust the consistency with more sherry if necessary to achieve a thick mustard sauce.
4. Store in lidded glass jars in the refrigerator for up to 2 months.

Always stir the sauce before measuring.

If Spicy Mustard Sauce becomes too thick as it sits in the refrigerator, you can thin it out with a little sherry. Speaking of sherry, I want you to use a good-quality medium-dry sherry. Good enough to serve to your best friend at 4 o'clock in the afternoon. One of my favorite brands is Savory and James Amontillado.

YIELDS approximately 1¾ cups

Quatre Fruits Sauce

Often an accompaniment to many Chinese appetizers, Quatre Fruits Sauce can be used as a glaze for roast ham, in marinades for barbecuing, and as a gift for a friend in place of flowers or a bottle of wine when you are arriving for dinner. It is also a crucial ingredient in Karen Lee's Five Spice Cocoa Cake.

1 cup Chinese plum sauce
1 cup peach preserves
1 cup apricot preserves
1½ cups unsweetened applesauce
2 tablespoons American chili sauce
2 tablespoons cognac

1. Using the on-and-off technique, combine all the ingredients in the bowl of a food processor until well blended.

2. Place the Quatre Fruits Sauce in lidded glass jars and refrigerate up to 4 months.

YIELDS approximately 5 cups

Tomato Sauce

This basic tomato sauce has become a staple to me for many cuisines. It is great to have on hand for French or Spanish cooking when a recipe calls for a few tablespoons of tomato sauce. I use it in Chinese cooking instead of the catsup that so many Chinese chefs use and in Italian cooking as a base for many pasta sauces.

The original recipe came from Lydie Marshall, who makes some of the best French food I have ever eaten. My variation includes the addition of the green part of the leek, an idea I got from Giuliano Bugialli, the well-known author and teacher of Italian cooking. He said that adding leeks gives a great flavor to tomato sauce. I tried it and agreed emphatically. Make big batches of this as it goes so fast.

4　cups canned Italian tomatoes (35-ounce can) or 3
　　pounds very ripe fresh tomatoes
1　medium-size leek
2　tablespoons olive oil
2　tablespoons sweet butter
1　tablespoon minced garlic
1　teaspoon sugar
　　Freshly ground black pepper (20 turns of the mill)

1. If using canned tomatoes, pass the tomatoes through a food mill into a bowl. Reserve the pureed tomatoes with their juice; discard the seeds. If using fresh tomatoes, dice them without peeling or seeding.

2. Remove the root end of the leek, then split the leek in half lengthwise all the way through. Place it under forcefully running warm water to remove all traces of sand. Mince the green part only (reserve the white part for use in other recipes). The yield should be 1 cup minced leeks.

3. In a 12-inch skillet, heat the olive oil and butter until the butter foams. Add the leeks and garlic; sauté over medium-low heat for about 5 minutes or until the leeks are limp.

4. Add the tomatoes, sugar, and pepper. Bring to a simmer over high heat. Stir well to combine. Turn the heat to low. Simmer uncovered for 1 hour or until the sauce has reduced by half. If using fresh tomatoes, pass the sauce through a food mill. Allow it to cool, then place the sauce in lidded glass jars. Refrigerate up to 1 week or freeze up to 6 months.

In the summertime and early fall, I use fresh tomatoes that I allow to ripen several days or up to a week. At all other times of the year, I use any good-quality canned tomatoes from the San Marzano region of Italy. It will say *San Marzano* on the label, and to me, the region is more important than the brand.

YIELDS 3 cups

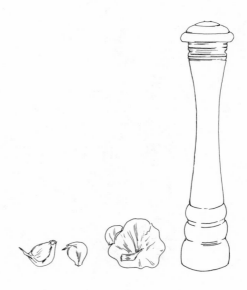

Appetizers and First Courses

WILD MUSHROOM SPRING ROLLS

SHANGHAI VEGETARIAN SPRING ROLLS

COCONUT SHRIMP

GOAT CHEESE WONTONS

LAMB AND ARUGULA SHAO MAI WITH
LEMON DIPPING SAUCE

CHINESE CHICKEN PÂTÉ

SKEWERED BARBECUED SHRIMP

BARBECUED RIBLETS OF BEEF

SHRIMP AND ICICLE RADISH TOAST

SKEWERED CHICKEN WITH PAPAYA RELISH

STUFFED ARTICHOKES WITH
PICKLED GINGER VINAIGRETTE

CHINESE CRAB CAKES

BEET AND SWEET POTATO TEMPURA

SCALLION GARLIC RICE CAKES

Wild Mushroom Spring Rolls

The filling for these spring rolls is so luscious that it is always hard to choose whether to make it into spring rolls or serve it as a vegetable dish. If you serve the filling as a vegetable accompaniment, do not place it in a strainer set over a bowl to drain as indicated in step 4. Instead, remove the contents from the wok to a serving dish.

Two kinds of fresh wild mushrooms are in the filling: chanterelles, and cremini, originally grown in the Po Valley in northern Italy. Frequently, cremini and chanterelles are not available at the same time, in which case you can use all cremini or all chanterelles for a total of 10 ounces of fresh mushrooms, which would yield 6 cups shredded.

½ cup dried porcini mushrooms

SEASONING SAUCE
1 tablespoon porcini stock (see step 1)
1 teaspoon water chestnut powder
1 tablespoon medium-dry sherry
1 tablespoon plus 1 teaspoon dark soy sauce
1 tablespoon plus 1 teaspoon oyster sauce

3 medium-size leeks
3 tablespoons peanut oil
6 ounces shredded fresh Italian mushrooms (cremini), approximately 4 cups
4 ounces shredded fresh French mushrooms (chanterelles), approximately 2 cups

10 to 12 Doll Spring Roll Shell wrappers, frozen
1 egg, beaten

3 cups peanut oil for deep-frying

1. Place the dried porcini mushrooms in a bowl and add 1 cup cold water. Soak for 1 hour, or until soft. Squeeze the porcini over the bowl then chop. Set aside. Pour the porcini liquid through a strainer lined with cheesecloth. Place the liquid in a saucepan and reduce to 1 tablespoon. Allow this porcini stock to cool.

2. Make the seasoning sauce by dissolving the water chestnut powder in the sherry. Add the porcini stock, soy sauce, and oyster sauce; mix until well combined.

3. Remove the root ends of the leeks, then split the leeks in half lengthwise all the way through. Place them under forcefully running warm water to remove all traces of sand. Then shred the white and also the tender light green parts (reserve the dark green part for Tomato Sauce or stock). The yield should be 3 cups shredded leeks.

4. Place a wok over high heat for about 1 minute or until it smokes. Add 3 tablespoons peanut oil and heat until hot but not smoking. Add the leeks and stir-fry 2 to 3 minutes or until they are limp. Add the porcini, cremini, and chanterelles. Stir-fry another minute. Restir the seasoning sauce and add it to the wok all at once, continuing to stir-fry until no liquid remains. This should take no longer than 3 more minutes. Empty the contents of the wok into a colander or wire strainer set over a bowl and allow to cool. The filling must be thoroughly cooled and drained otherwise it will break the wrappers.

5. While the spring roll filling is cooling, remove the spring roll wrappers from the freezer and wrap them in a damp tea towel. When they have defrosted, separate them, then pile them back up on top of each other like a stack of pancakes and wrap them once again in the damp tea towel. If the wrappers dry out, they are useless. This will happen if they are exposed to air for more than a few minutes.

6. *To Wrap the Spring Rolls:* Take a square spring roll wrapper and angle it on a flat surface so that it faces you in a diamond shape. Take about ¼ cup of filling and place it in the lower center of the diamond. Shape it like a thick cigar. Holding the filling firmly with the last 3 fingers of both hands, take the corner of the diamond nearest you and fold it tightly over the filling. Be sure to

push the filling toward you while you are folding the corner of the wrapper away from you. Make another fold away from you, doubling over the filling, always pressing in toward the flat working surface. With beaten egg on your fingertips, generously moisten the 3 remaining points of the diamond (the diamond has now been folded in half, so the 3 points are part of the remaining triangle).

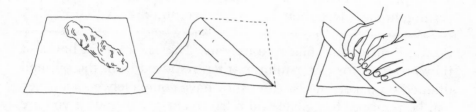

Take the 2 side points and fold them in toward the bottom center, folding the left one in first and then the right one. Make sure there is an overlap of at least 1 inch. At this point, the spring roll should resemble a bulging envelope. Take the bottom edge of the envelope—the edge nearest you—and roll it away from you for 2 complete turns. Again make sure that you press the filling in tightly. Bring the remaining free corner over and seal the moistened tip onto the roll.

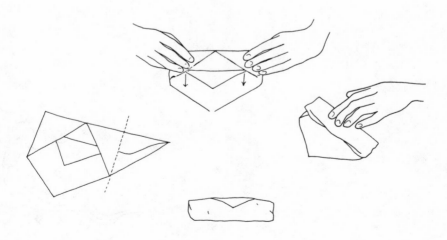

7. *To Fry the Spring Rolls.* Heat the wok until it smokes. Add 3 cups of oil and heat until the oil reaches 350°. Fry the spring rolls 5 at a time for about 3 minutes or until they are golden brown. Turn once. Drain well on paper towels before serving. Cut them in half once on the diagonal, then arrange the spring rolls on a serving platter.

Doll Spring Roll Shells are usually purchased frozen. When returning home, place them in your freezer until ready to use.

Spring Rolls can be made entirely in advance (up to 24 hours) if they are fried for just 1 minute, then removed from the oil, and drained on paper towels. After they have completely cooled, they can be removed to a plate and refrigerated uncovered. If you are making them only several hours in advance, it is not necessary to refrigerate after this preliminary frying. Before serving, fry as in step 7.

YIELDS 10 spring rolls

Shanghai Vegetarian Spring Rolls

The difference between spring rolls and egg rolls is primarily the wrapper. The spring roll wrapper is much thinner and crispier. The difference between the filling in these spring rolls and that in traditional ones is the absence of meat.

2 cups mung bean sprouts
⅓ cup dried Chinese mushrooms

SEASONING SAUCE
1 tablespoon mushroom stock (see step 2)
2 teaspoons water chestnut powder
1 tablespoon medium-dry sherry
1 tablespoon oyster sauce
2 tablespoons dark soy sauce

2 medium-size leeks
2 tablespoons peanut oil
½ cup shredded winter bamboo shoots
½ cup shredded red sweet pepper
½ cup shredded yellow Holland pepper
2 cups shredded bok choy, white and green parts included

10 Doll Spring Roll Shell wrappers, frozen
1 egg, beaten

3 cups peanut oil for deep-frying

1. Place the bean sprouts on paper towels to dry.
2. Rinse the mushrooms under cold running water. In a small bowl, soak them in cold water to cover for about 1 hour or until soft. Squeeze them over the bowl. Remove the stems and shred the mushrooms. Set the mushrooms aside. Place the stems

in a saucepan. Add the mushroom liquid. Reduce until about 1 tablespoon remains. Strain the mushroom stock, then allow it to cool. Discard the stems.

3. Make the seasoning sauce by first dissolving the water chestnut powder in the sherry, then adding the mushroom stock, oyster sauce, and soy sauce. Stir until well combined.

4. Remove the root ends of the leeks, then split the leeks in half lengthwise all the way through. Place them under forcefully running warm water to remove all traces of sand. Then shred the white and also the tender light green parts into 3-inch strips (reserve the dark green part for Tomato Sauce, or stock). The yield should be 2 cups shredded leeks.

5. Place a wok over high heat for about 1 minute or until it smokes. Add the bean sprouts. Allow them to scorch on one side for approximately 30 seconds, shaking the wok occasionally. Flip the bean sprouts in the wok and scorch them on the other side for another 30 seconds. Turn off the heat. Remove the bean sprouts to a plate.

6. Return the wok to high heat. Add 2 tablespoons of peanut oil around the sides of the wok and heat for a few seconds. Add the leeks and stir-fry 1 minute. Add the mushrooms and the bamboo shoots, continuing to stir-fry another minute. Add the red and yellow peppers, stir-frying another minute. Restir the seasoning sauce and add it to the wok all at once, continuing to stir-fry. Add the bok choy. Stir-fry another minute or until the seasoning sauce has thickened and the vegetables have been glazed with the sauce. There should be no excess liquid. Empty the contents of the wok into a large wire strainer set over a bowl to catch the drippings. Allow to cool thoroughly. The filling must be dry and cool, otherwise it will break the wrappers.

7. While the spring roll filling is cooling, remove the spring roll wrappers from the freezer and wrap them in a damp tea towel. When they have defrosted, separate them, then pile them back up on top of each other like a stack of pancakes. Wrap them once again in the damp tea towel. If the wrappers dry out, they are useless. This will happen if they are exposed to air for more than a few minutes.

8. *To Wrap the Spring Rolls:* as described in Wild Mushroom Spring Rolls (see pp. 22–24).

9. *To Fry the Spring Rolls:* Heat the wok until it smokes. Add the 3 cups of peanut oil and heat until the oil reaches 350°. Fry the spring rolls 5 at a time for about 3 minutes or until they are golden brown. Turn once. Drain well on paper towels before serving. Cut them in half on the diagonal, then arrange the spring rolls on a serving platter.

Winter bamboo shoots are usually purchased in a can. Once opened, the leftover portion should be placed in a wide-mouthed glass jar and covered with water. In Chinese markets they are displayed in an open pail, allowing you to buy just the amount you need.

Spring Rolls can be made entirely in advance (up to 24 hours) if they are fried for just 1 minute, then removed from the oil, and drained on paper towels. After they have completely cooled, they can be removed to a plate and refrigerated uncovered. If you are making them only several hours in advance, it is not necessary to refrigerate after this preliminary frying. Before serving, fry as in step 9.

YIELDS 10 spring rolls

Coconut Shrimp

Joan Green developed this recipe and gave it to me. She is a supportive, adventurous lady who is also a long-time student and friend.

BATTER
2 eggs
1 egg yolk
2 tablespoons cornstarch
1 tablespoon medium-dry sherry

1 pound medium shrimp (21–25 to the pound)

MARINADE
1 tablespoon medium-dry sherry
1 tablespoon light soy sauce
1 teaspoon Oriental sesame oil

COCONUT MIXTURE
2 ounces sesame bread sticks
1½ cups sweetened coconut flakes
1½ teaspoons curry powder

3 cups peanut oil for deep-frying

1. Make the batter by combining the eggs, egg yolk, cornstarch, and sherry in a bowl. Beat until smooth. Refrigerate the batter uncovered for at least 1 hour or up to 12 hours.
2. *To Butterfly the Shrimp (see illustration, page 173):* Remove the shell, except for the last segment of the tail. Cut the shrimp along the convex side, but do not let the knife go all the way through the meat. With the tip of a boning knife, make a widthwise slit about 1 inch long in the middle of the shrimp on the convex side. Push the tail of the shrimp into the slit, then pull the

tail through to the other side. The purpose of butterflying is to prevent the shrimp from curling when cooked. Rinse, drain, and dry the shrimp.

3. Make the marinade by mixing together the sherry, soy sauce, and sesame oil. Stir until well combined. Marinate the shrimp for 1 hour or up to 12 hours in the refrigerator.

4. Make the coconut mixture by first placing the sesame bread sticks in a processor or blender. Process until pulverized. Measure out ½ cup ground sesame bread stick crumbs, and combine with coconut flakes and curry powder in a bowl.

5. Remove the shrimp from the refrigerator 30 minutes before frying and place them on several layers of paper towels. Spread the shrimp out so that they are in a single layer. Place a wok over high heat for about 1 minute or until it smokes. Add the peanut oil and heat until the oil reaches 350°. Stir the batter well to redistribute the cornstarch. Take each shrimp by the tail and dip it first in the batter and then in the coconut mixture. Coat all the shrimp before beginning the frying procedure. Place 6 shrimp in the wok. Deep-fry for 1 to 1½ minutes or until they are golden. Turn once. Remove the shrimp from the wok to a cookie sheet lined with paper towels. Repeat the procedure, deep-frying 6 shrimp at a time, until all are cooked. Serve immediately.

This dish is great for parties as the entire preparation can be done in advance and refrigerated, in which case remove the shrimp from the refrigerator 30 minutes prior to frying.

SERVES 4 to 5

Goat Cheese Wontons

The birth of this book began with my editor, Lindley Boegehold, saying to me, "Be as extreme as you like in pairing French and Chinese ingredients. I don't care if you stuff wontons with goat cheese."

Goat Cheese Wontons is a fabulous appetizer for all types of dinners. The filling also works well in phyllo dough, in omelets, or as a spread on good coarse-grain bread.

  2 teaspoons minced fresh rosemary
  1 tablespoon olive oil
  7 ounces mild goat cheese
1½ tablespoons diced sun-dried tomatoes
  2 teaspoons olive paste
30 thin square wonton wrappers
  1 egg, beaten
  3 cups peanut oil for deep-frying

1. Mix the fresh rosemary and olive oil in a small cup and allow to stand for 1 hour. In a medium bowl, mix together the goat cheese, rosemary-olive mixture, sun-dried tomatoes, and olive paste. Stir until well combined. Refrigerate for at least 6 hours.

2. *To Wrap the Wontons:* Working with 1 at a time, place a wonton wrapper in front of you so that it looks like a diamond shape. Center a teaspoon of filling on the wrapper. Moisten the 2 sides furthest away from you with beaten egg. As if making a triangle, fold the bottom half of the wrapper upward over the filling. Do not align the 2 upper tips but rather let this corner fall to the

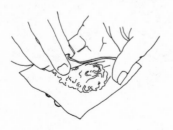

right of the upper point of the triangle. Pinch together each bottom corner of the triangle, then draw these 2 corners downward and inward until they meet at the base. Using your fingers, seal both sides. Overlap and seal with beaten egg the tips of the 2 corners. Pinch them together.

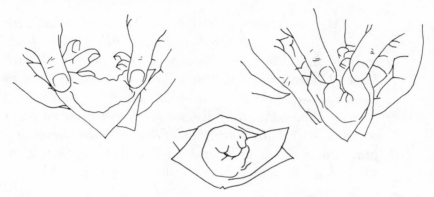

3. Place the filled wontons on greased plates and refrigerate 1 hour. The purpose of refrigerating is to keep the cheese filling from overheating and oozing out of the skins when they cook.

4. Heat a wok until it smokes. Add peanut oil and heat until it reaches 350°. Fry wontons 6 to 8 at a time for about 30 seconds, turning once. Drain on paper towels and serve immediately.

Goat Cheese Wontons can be prepared early in the day through step 3.

When buying wonton wrappers, try to buy the thin ones. They are available in Chinese markets. Once purchased, if you are not using them within a few days, they should be frozen double-wrapped, first in plastic wrap, next in aluminum foil, and then placed in a plastic bag. This protection will prevent the ends from drying out.

If the wonton wrappers are not paper thin, roll each one individually with a rolling pin.

YIELDS approximately 30 wontons

Lamb and Arugula Shao Mai With Lemon Dipping Sauce

Shao Mai are steamed dumplings. These are filled with lamb, whereas traditional ones are filled with pork, shrimp, and bok choy. Because lemon pairs well with lamb, I have chosen a lemon dipping sauce to go with them instead of the usual soy-based sauce.

When the dumplings have finished steaming, I center a little white soufflé dish filled with the lemon dipping sauce on one layer of a bamboo steamer, then place the bamboo layer on a bamboo tray for serving.

¼ cup dried porcini mushrooms
1 tablespoon reduced porcini stock (see step 1)
1 bunch arugula
1 tablespoon water chestnut powder
1 tablespoon medium-dry sherry
1 tablespoon dark soy sauce
1 teaspoon Oriental sesame oil
1 egg yolk
½ pound ground lamb
1 teaspoon minced garlic
1 tablespoon minced shallots
30 thin square wonton wrappers

LEMON DIPPING SAUCE
1 tablespoon plus 2 teaspoons fresh lemon juice
1 tablespoon Dijon mustard
3 tablespoons olive oil

Kale leaves

Special Equipment
Cheesecloth

1. Place the mushrooms in a small bowl, cover with cold water, and soak for about 30 minutes, or until soft. Squeeze them over the bowl. Strain the liquid into a saucepan and reduce until 1 tablespoon remains. Dice the porcini.

2. While the arugula is still tied, cut off and discard 2 inches of the stems. Wash, spin-dry, then chop the arugula.

3. In a bowl, dissolve the water chestnut powder in the sherry. Mix in the soy sauce, sesame oil, and egg yolk. Add to this mixture the ground lamb, porcini, porcini stock, arugula, garlic, and shallots. Using a bunch of bamboo chopsticks (Chinese wire whisk), stir well.

4. *To Wrap the Wontons:* Place a wonton wrapper in the palm of your hand. Put 1 tablespoon of the filling in the center of the wrapper. Gather the 4 sides of the wrapper around the filling, letting them pleat naturally and meet in the center, so that you have 4 loops. Then, using the thumb and index finger of your other hand, push each large pleat into several smaller pleats. To pack the filling tightly, squeeze in the finished pouch slightly above the center. Flatten out the bottom by tapping gently on the table (this makes it stand upright).

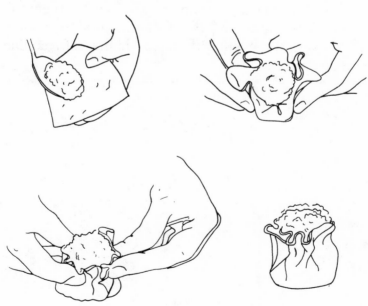

5. Use a stainless steel wok or a pot that is approximately the same diameter as the bamboo steamer you are using. Fill the wok with water to a depth of 2 or 3 inches. Line 2 or 3 levels of the bamboo steamer with cheesecloth that has been wrung out in cold water. Place the dumplings on top of the cheesecloth and steam over high heat for 6 minutes.

6. While the dumplings are steaming, make the lemon dipping sauce by mixing together the lemon juice, mustard, and olive oil. Beat with a bunch of chopsticks until the sauce has thickened.

7. Remove the dumplings and the cheesecloth, then surround the levels of the bamboo steamer with kale. Distribute the dumplings evenly in the bamboo steamer. Steam the dumplings 1 more minute. Serve in the bamboo steamer with lemon dipping sauce.

If you can't find thin wonton wrappers, roll each wrapper with a rolling pin to make it thinner.

These dumplings and the accompanying dipping sauce can be prepared early in the day through step 6. Remove them to a plate and cover them with a damp cheesecloth so that the tips don't dry out. If you are using them within a few hours, refrigerating them is not necessary.

YIELDS 30 dumplings

Chinese Chicken Pâté

Less rich than many of the pork-based pâtés, this Oriental version of a French pâté will definitely impress your guests, not only with its taste but also with its aesthetic appeal, for when it is cut into serving slices, the layers of red pepper and green long beans reveal a beautiful pattern.

Chinese Chicken Pâté only takes about an hour to put together, plus baking time, but it must be done a day ahead.

1 sweet red pepper
10 Chinese long beans
5 to 6 large bok choy leaves
1 pound ground chicken breast
½ cup corn oil
¼ cup Chinese red vinegar
1½ teaspoons salt
Freshly ground black pepper (20 turns of the mill)
⅓ cup sliced (⅛-inch rounds) scallions, white and green parts included
1 egg, beaten
2 tablespoons Pickled Ginger (see pp. 134–135)
1 teaspoon Hot Sauce (see p. 10–11)

Butter for greasing

1. *To Roast the Pepper, Method 1, for on top of a gas range:* Place the whole pepper directly on the heating element of the stove. Turn the heat to the lowest possible flame. Roast the pepper, occasionally turning with tongs as the skin begins to char. Turn every 5 minutes or so until the entire pepper has charred— the more charred, the easier it will be to peel. Using the lowest possible heat, this will take about 20 to 30 minutes.

Method 2, for the broiling unit whether gas or electric: Preheat the oven to broil. Place the pepper on a rack resting on a shallow roasting pan or a cookie sheet that has been lined with aluminum foil. Broil the pepper 3 inches from the heat source, turning occasionally. Char all sides of the pepper. This will take from 10 to 20 minutes.

2. Place the charred pepper in a brown paper bag for 10 minutes. When it "sweats," the skin loosens, which makes peeling it easier. Remove the pepper from the paper bag. Cut out the pepper's stem and discard. Quarter, core, and seed the pepper. Using a knife, scrape off the charred skin. Cut the peeled pepper into long, thin strips.

3. Steam the Chinese long beans for 3 minutes or until they have softened but still have some crunch. Remove them from the steamer. To stop the cooking and hold the color, plunge the long beans into a bowl of ice-cold water for about a minute or until they cool. Drain the long beans in a colander set over a bowl. After they are dry, remove the stem ends.

4. Steam the bok choy leaves for 1 minute. Plunge them into a bowl of ice-cold water, then drain.

5. In a large bowl, blend the chicken with the corn oil, vinegar, salt, pepper, scallions, egg, Pickled Ginger, and Hot Sauce. Mix well.

6. Preheat the oven to 350°. Grease a loaf pan that is 7⅜ inches long by 3⅝ inches wide by 2½ inches deep. Line the pan with overlapping steamed bok choy leaves, draping the leaves over the sides of the pan, completely covering the bottom and sides.

7. Take ¾ cup of the chicken mixture and spread it with a rubber spatula as evenly as possible over the bok choy leaves in the loaf pan.

8. Cut the long beans the size of the length of the pan. Arrange 9 or 10 long beans in a row lengthwise. Add another ½ cup of the chicken mixture and spread it evenly over the long beans.

9. Patch the strips of roasted pepper, arranging them in long rows lengthwise over the chicken mixture. Spread the rest of the chicken mixture gently over the peppers, so as not to disturb the preceding layers.

10. Fold the overlapping layers of bok choy leaves to cover the pâté. Tap the pan on the table a few times to eliminate air bubbles, then cover with aluminum foil.

11. Place the loaf pan in a shallow roasting pan filled with boiling water to a depth of 1½ inches. Bake for 45 minutes. Remove the pâté from the oven and allow to cool for 1 hour. Unmold the pâté onto a plate and refrigerate for 1 day. When ready to serve, remove the pâté from the refrigerator 30 minutes before serving. Cut into slices for individual servings.

For the Chinese long beans, you can substitute approximately 30 string beans.

SERVES 8

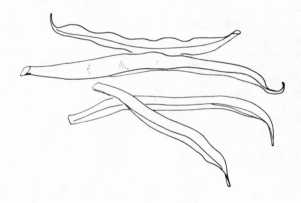

Skewered Barbecued Shrimp

Shrimp still remains the most popular seafood in America. When you marinate them with this tangy Chinese-American Sauce then barbecue them on a charcoal grill, you will definitely have a hit on your hands.

¾ pound medium shrimp (21–25 to the pound)

BARBECUE SAUCE
1 tablespoon peanut oil
2 teaspoons minced ginger
1 teaspoon minced garlic
5 tablespoons Tomato Sauce (see pp. 16–17)
3 tablespoons medium-dry sherry
3 tablespoons dark brown sugar
2 tablespoons dark soy sauce
1 tablespoon red wine vinegar
1 teaspoon Hot Sauce (see pp. 10–11)

Special Equipment
Bamboo skewers

1. Shell, devein, rinse, drain, and dry the shrimp on paper towels.

2. Place a wok over high heat for about 1 minute or until it smokes. Add the peanut oil and heat a few seconds. Add the ginger, then turn the heat to low and stir a few seconds. Add the garlic. Continue to stir another few seconds. Add the tomato sauce, sherry, sugar, soy sauce, vinegar, and Hot Sauce. Turn the heat to high and allow the sauce to come to a boil, stirring for about another minute or until the sauce has thickened. Remove the sauce from the wok and allow it to cool.

3. Place the shrimp in the barbecue sauce. Marinate them in the refrigerator for at least 2 hours or up to 8 hours.

4. Place the bamboo skewers in a bowl of water and allow to soak for 30 minutes. This will prevent them from burning.

5. Prepare a charcoal grill or preheat the broiler for at least 15 minutes.

6. Remove the bamboo skewers from the water. Skewer 3 to 4 shrimp on each. Grill or broil the shrimp for about 1 to 2 minutes on each side or until they are cooked through. Serve immediately.

This barbecue sauce is also wonderful on steak, chicken, and pork.

SERVES 2 to 3

Barbecued Riblets of Beef

These short ribs seasoned with a Chinese marinade taste best grilled outdoors over American mesquite although you can broil them indoors as well.
The ribs marinate overnight, so plan accordingly.

2 pounds short ribs (flanken), lean and meaty

MARINADE
2 tablespoons brown sugar
2 tablespoons light soy sauce
1 tablespoon medium-dry sherry
1 tablespoon Oriental sesame oil
2 tablespoons unhulled sesame seeds
2 teaspoons minced garlic
1 teaspoon minced ginger
2 whole scallions, cut into ⅛-inch rounds
Freshly ground black pepper (10 turns of the mill)

Quatre Fruits Sauce (see page 15)
Spicy Mustard Sauce (see page 14)

Garnish
Watercress

1. Have the butcher cut the short ribs into small pieces, ½ inch thick by 1½ inches wide by 2 inches long.
2. Trim the fat and gristle from the outside of the ribs. Score each rib 3 times on both sides.
3. Make the marinade by mixing together the sugar, soy sauce, sherry, sesame oil, sesame seeds, garlic, ginger, scallions, and pepper. Stir until well combined.
4. Place the ribs in a shallow rectangular pan and pour the marinade over them. Turn the ribs over in the marinade, making sure that the marinade touches all surfaces and cuts. Marinate for 24 hours in the refrigerator, turning the ribs from time to time.

5. *To Barbecue on an Outdoor Grill, Method 1:* Remove the ribs from the refrigerator. If you have them, soak 2 handfuls of mesquite chips or 2 to 3 pieces of mesquite wood for 1 hour in water. After 30 minutes, make a charcoal fire. Let the coals burn for 30 to 40 minutes, then add the drained mesquite.

Place the ribs on top of the grill rack. Cover the barbecue, making sure the vent is wide open. Grill the ribs for about 10 minutes on each side or until they are seared and cooked through.

To Barbecue Under the Broiler, Method 2: Remove the ribs from the refrigerator. Place them on a rack set over the broiling pan. Preheat the broiler for 30 minutes. Broil the ribs 2 inches from the flame for 20 minutes, turning once at midpoint.

6. Serve immediately with Quatre Fruits Sauce and Spicy Mustard Sauce. Garnish with watercress.

SERVES 4 to 6

Shrimp and Icicle Radish Toast

Here's a fresh look at shrimp toast, combining icicle radish (also known as daikon or Chinese turnip) and challah, which is a traditional Jewish braided egg bread.

½ pound shrimp
1 tablespoon water chestnut powder
½ tablespoon dark soy sauce
1 teaspoon medium-dry sherry
1 egg yolk
¼ cup minced icicle radish
2 teaspoons minced ginger
2 whole scallions, cut into ⅛-inch rounds
½ teaspoon salt
Freshly ground white pepper (10 turns of the mill)
½ teaspoon sugar
4 to 5 slices challah bread
2 tablespoons unhulled sesame seeds
3 cups peanut oil for deep-frying
Quatre Fruits Sauce (see page 15)
Spicy Mustard Sauce (see page 14)

GARNISH
Watercress *or*
Deep-fried Bok Choy Leaves (see page 132)

1. Shell, devein, rinse, drain, and dry the shrimp on paper towels. Mince the shrimp.
2. Dissolve the water chestnut powder in the soy sauce and the sherry. Add this mixture to the minced shrimp, along with the egg yolk, icicle radish, ginger, scallions, salt, pepper, and sugar.
3. Holding several chopsticks in one hand (the Chinese version of a wire whisk) or a wooden spoon, stir the shrimp mixture until it is well combined. Refrigerate for at least 1 hour, or up to 24 hours.

4. Lay the bread out to dry on a flat surface for 2 hours. Turn each piece over and allow to sit for another 2 hours.

5. Using an icing spatula, spread the shrimp mixture evenly over the slices of bread. Sprinkle a few sesame seeds on top, then cut each piece into quarters. (If you are not deep-frying immediately, refrigerate for up to 3 hours, then remove from the refrigerator 30 minutes before cooking.)

6. Place a wok over high heat for about 1 minute or until it smokes. Pour in the oil. Heat the oil to 350°. Holding a piece of the bread in your fingers, gently lower it into the oil with the shrimp side down. Fry 12 pieces at a time. After about 1 minute, turn them over with chopsticks and fry another minute or until the toast has turned golden brown. Using a wire strainer, lift the shrimp toast out of the oil and let drain on several layers of paper towel. Repeat with the remaining 12 pieces. Serve immediately with Quatre Fruits Sauce and Spicy Mustard Sauce. Garnish with watercress or deep-fried bok choy leaves.

YIELDS 16 to 20 pieces

Skewered Chicken with Papaya Relish

This makes an interesting as well as hearty appetizer.

MARINADE

One 1-inch chunk ginger
- 1 tablespoon light soy sauce
- 1 tablespoon medium-dry sherry
- 1 tablespoon Oriental sesame oil
  Freshly ground black pepper (10 turns of the mill)

- 1 pound boneless, skinless chicken breasts, trimmed and cut into thick strips

- 1 medium-size well-ripened papaya, peeled and diced (about 2 cups)
- 2 medium-size Granny Smith apples, peeled and diced (about 2 cups)
- ½ cup chopped red onion

DRESSING 1

- 1 tablespoon plus 1 teaspoon Japanese rice vinegar
- ½ teaspoon salt
- ¼ cup corn oil
  Freshly ground black pepper (10 turns of the mill)

- 1 icicle radish, peeled and shredded (about 2 cups)
- ⅔ cup finely shredded red sweet pepper
- ⅔ cup finely shredded yellow Holland pepper

DRESSING 2

- 1 tablespoon Japanese rice vinegar
- ½ teaspoon salt
- 3 tablespoons corn oil
  Freshly ground black pepper (10 turns of the mill)

Special Equipment
Bamboo skewers

1. Cut the ginger in half (peeling is not necessary), then place it in a garlic press. Extract the juice over a bowl large enough to hold the marinade and the chicken. Place the soy sauce, sherry, sesame oil, and pepper in the bowl. Stir until well combined. Add the chicken and marinate for 1 hour.

2. Place the papaya, apple, and onion in a bowl. Mix well.

3. Combine the ingredients for Dressing 1 by first placing the vinegar in a bowl and then adding the salt, stirring until it dissolves. Mix in the oil and pepper. Add this dressing to the papaya mixture. Allow to marinate for 1 hour.

4. Place the icicle radish and red and yellow peppers in a bowl.

5. Combine the ingredients for Dressing 2 by first placing the vinegar in a bowl and then adding the salt, stirring until it dissolves. Mix in the corn oil and pepper. Add this dressing to the icicle radish mixture. Toss well. Allow to marinate 1 hour.

6. Preheat the oven to broil. Place the marinated chicken on 4 or 5 bamboo skewers, doubling the chicken over so that it will be thick. Broil the chicken as close to the flame as possible for 4 to 6 minutes, or until it is cooked through.

7. Choose a flat serving platter. Place the icicle radish mixture in the center. Place the papaya mixture on 2 sides around it and the skewered chicken on the other 2 sides, jutting out like spokes of a wheel. Serve immediately.

Buy your papaya 5 to 7 days in advance, so that it is sure to ripen and be sweet.

The chicken will taste even better grilled outdoors.

Icicle radish is also called daikon or Chinese turnip. They generally run quite large so choose a small one.

SERVES 4

Stuffed Artichokes with Pickled Ginger Vinaigrette

I happen to love artichokes. This recipe uses the Western concept of stuffing artichokes, in this case with Chinese ingredients. As part of the stuffing, I chose a favorite Chinese ingredient, bean curd. Low in calories and cholesterol and high in protein, bean curd is called "meat without bones" by the Chinese.

I like to serve these artichokes as a first course or light lunch. The dressing is so good you can use it on your regular salad greens without the bean curd.

4 medium-size fresh artichokes

PICKLED GINGER VINAIGRETTE DRESSING
3 tablespoons Chinese red vinegar
1½ teaspoons salt
2 teaspoons Spicy Mustard Sauce (see page 14)
6 tablespoons corn oil
3 tablespoons olive oil
3 tablespoons sliced (⅛-inch rounds) scallions, white and green parts included
1 tablespoon minced Pickled Ginger (see pp. 134–135)
1 teaspoon minced garlic
1 fresh bean curd cake (3 ounces), diced

1. Wash the artichokes, then slice approximately 1½ inches off the top of each. Remove about 1 inch of the stem, enough that each artichoke stands upright. Scissor off the tip of each artichoke leaf.

2. Place the artichokes in an upright position in a steamer. Depending on their size, steam them for 15 to 30 minutes or until one of the lower leaves pulls out easily. Remove them from the

steamer. To stop the cooking and hold the color, plunge the artichokes into a bowl of ice-cold water for about a minute or until they cool. Turn them upside down on a rack and allow to drain.

3. Once drained, scoop out the center of each artichoke with a serrated grapefruit spoon. Remove only the small prickly leaves and the fuzzy part beneath them. Be careful to leave the artichoke heart intact.

4. Make the Pickled Ginger Vinaigrette Dressing by mixing together the vinegar, salt, and Spicy Mustard Sauce. Stir until the salt is dissolved, then add the corn oil and olive oil, beating slowly until the mixture has thickened. Add the scallions, Pickled Ginger, and garlic. Beat until well combined. Stir in the bean curd.

5. Turn the artichokes upright and place them on a platter. Spoon the dressing into the center cavity and around the artichokes. Serve at room temperature.

Both the artichokes and the dressing can be prepared early in the day; however, they should not be combined until 30 minutes before serving.

SERVES 4

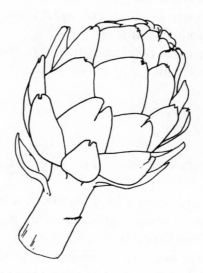

Chinese Crab Cakes

With an Oriental touch of bok choy, rice, hoisin sauce, Spicy Mustard Sauce, and coriander, these crab cakes are my Nouvelle Chinese version of an all-time American favorite.

1 pound lump crabmeat
4 ounces sesame bread sticks
1 cup chopped bok choy, white and green parts included
1 cup cooked Kokuho Rose rice
2 eggs, beaten
1 tablespoon Spicy Mustard Sauce (see page 14)
½ teaspoon Worcestershire sauce
1 teaspoon dark soy sauce
2 teaspoons hoisin sauce
⅓ cup mayonnaise
¼ cup sliced (⅛-inch rounds) scallions, white and green
    parts included
2 tablespoons chopped coriander leaves
5 tablespoons peanut oil
2 medium-size Belgian endive, split and cut into strips
1 bunch arugula

Special Equipment
Cheesecloth

1. Pick over crabmeat to remove all traces of cartilage and shell.
2. Place the sesame bread sticks in a processor or blender. Using the pulse technique, process until pulverized. Measure out 1 cup ground bread crumbs.
3. Place the bok choy in a piece of cheesecloth that has been wrung out in cold water. Squeeze hard to extract the excess moisture. Place the bok choy in a bowl, along with the cooked rice,

eggs, Spicy Mustard Sauce, Worcestershire, soy sauce, hoisin sauce, mayonnaise, scallions, and coriander leaves. Stir with chopsticks until well combined, then fold in the crabmeat.

4. Shape the mixture into 10 (½ cup each) equal-size round crab cakes. Coat each crab cake with bread crumbs. Refrigerate for at least 1 hour or up to 12 hours.

5. When ready to fry, place a 12-inch cast-iron or stainless steel skillet over high heat for about 1 minute. Add 4 tablespoons of the peanut oil and heat until hot but not smoking. Add 5 crab cakes and cook over medium-high heat for 3 minutes, turning once at midpoint. The crab cakes should be browned well on both sides. Using a spatula, remove the crab cakes from the skillet. Add the remaining 1 tablespoon peanut oil and sauté the remaining 5 crab cakes.

6. Arrange the Belgian endive and arugula on a flat serving dish. Place the crab cakes on top. Serve immediately.

For the Kokuho Rose rice, which is a short-grained Japanese rice, any cooked rice can be substituted.

SERVES 4 to 5

Beet and Sweet Potato Tempura

The secret to perfect results with this batter is to have the oil hot and the batter cold. Deep-fry one vegetable round for a test. If the batter is too thick, you can add an ice cube, which makes it at once colder and thinner. The recipe can be made early in the day (through step 4), but the vegetables must be fried at the last minute. You can serve Beet and Sweet Potato Tempura as a first course at dinner or as an appetizer on bamboo skewers at a cocktail party.

BATTER
½ cup flour
⅓ cup cornstarch
1 teaspoon salt
1 tablespoon Oriental sesame oil
1 teaspoon dark soy sauce
⅔ cup beer, cold and flat
2 teaspoons double-acting baking powder

1 bunch watercress
4 small to medium-size beets
1 medium-size to large sweet potato
3 cups peanut oil for deep-frying

GARNISH
1 lime, cut into 6 wedges

1. *To Make the Batter:* Place the flour, cornstarch, and salt in a bowl. Mix with several chopsticks. Combine the sesame oil, soy sauce, and beer in a second bowl. Add this liquid all at once to the dry ingredients, mixing until the batter is almost smooth. Add the baking powder and mix again. Refrigerate uncovered for at least 4 hours or up to 12 hours.

2. While the watercress is still tied, cut off and discard 2 inches of the stems. Wash the watercress, then spin-dry.

3. Separate the beet roots from the greens, leaving at least 3 inches of the stem on the root ends. Reserve the greens for another use. Scrub the beets and the sweet potato.

4. Steam the beets and the sweet potato for 15 minutes. Peel, then cut them into thick rounds, a little more than ¼ inch.

5. Place a wok over high heat for about 1 minute or until it smokes. Add the peanut oil and heat until it reaches 350°. Dip the beets and the sweet potato rounds, one at a time, into the batter. Place up to 6 rounds in the wok and deep-fry for about 2 minutes or until they are golden brown. Remove the rounds from the wok with a wire strainer and drain on several layers of paper towels. Repeat this procedure until all the tempura is cooked.

6. Place the tempura on a bed of watercress and garnish with lime wedges.

SERVES 4

Scallion Garlic Rice Cakes

These are the rice cakes that usually go with classic Chinese dishes such as Sizzling Shrimp on Rice Patties, or Sizzling Rice Soup. Now they are an appetizer. I think of them as the Chinese answer to garlic bread. Perfect to munch on at the cocktail hour.

   1 cup raw Chinese sweet rice
   1 teaspoon Oriental sesame oil
1¼ cups cold water
   2 cups peanut oil for deep-frying
   ½ teaspoon salt
   2 tablespoons sweet butter
   2 tablespoons minced garlic
1½ cups sliced (⅛-inch rounds) scallions, white and green
      parts included

1. Preheat the oven to 375°.

2. Place the rice in a strainer and rinse under cold running water. Allow to drain. Grease an 8-inch square brownie pan with the sesame oil. Pour the cold water in the pan, then add the rice. Shake the pan to level the rice in the water. Cover it with foil. Bake the rice on the middle rack of the oven for 30 minutes. Remove the foil. Reduce the oven temperature to 300° and continue to bake for another 1½ to 2 hours or until the rice is dry enough to remove from the pan easily with a spatula.

3. With your hands, break the rice into uneven 1½-inch squares.

4. Place a wok over high heat for about 1 minute or until it smokes. Add the peanut oil and heat until the oil reaches 375° or until bubbles form rapidly around a chopstick that you stand in the middle of the wok. Slide about 5 rice squares into the wok. Deep-fry the rice squares in the hot oil for about 30 seconds, then turn them over and deep-fry another 30 seconds or until they puff up and become brown and crisp. Remove them from the oil with

a wire strainer. Drain them well on several layers of paper towels. Repeat the frying procedure until all the rice cakes have been fried. Sprinkle the rice cakes with salt.

5. In a small skillet, heat the butter until it foams. Add the garlic and sauté over low heat until it has lightly browned. Add the scallions and sauté over medium heat another minute or two or until they have wilted. Turn off the heat. Spoon about ½ teaspoon of the garlic/scallion mixture onto each rice cake, then place the rice cakes on a serving dish and serve immediately or at room temperature, in which case they can be made several hours in advance.

Sweet rice, also called glutinous or sticky rice, is a short-grain rice that can be purchased in Chinese groceries.

YIELDS approximately 25 rice cakes

Salads

CHINESE COLESLAW

BEET AND WATER CHESTNUT SALAD

STRING BEAN SALAD WITH
DOUBLE SESAME DRESSING

LONG BEAN, ROASTED PEPPER, AND
GOAT CHEESE SALAD

JICAMA AND DANDELION SALAD

CELERY ROOT, SNOW PEA, AND
RADICCHIO SALAD

SPRING GINGER CRAB SALAD

BARBECUED ROAST DUCK SALAD

SICHUAN CHICKEN SALAD

SCALLOP SALAD

Chinese Coleslaw

This Eastern version of an American favorite side dish combines purple cabbage with Chinese Napa cabbage in a sweet and spicy Oriental dressing.

One 2-pound Chinese Napa cabbage
One 2-pound purple cabbage
   3 tablespoons salt
  ¼ cup peanut oil
  ¼ cup minced Pickled Ginger (see pp. 134–135)
  ⅔ cup Japanese rice vinegar
  6 tablespoons sugar
  4 whole scallions, cut into ⅛-inch rounds
  ¼ cup chopped coriander leaves
  2 teaspoons Chili Oil (see page 9)
  2 tablespoons Oriental sesame oil

1. Split the cabbages in half. Remove the cores and discard. Shred the cabbages. Place the shredded cabbage on a large plate and toss with salt. Cover with paper towels. Place a heavy, flat weight, such as an iron skillet, over the paper towels and let stand for about 2 hours. Squeeze the liquid from the cabbage with your hands and discard.

2. Place a wok over high heat for about 1 minute or until it smokes. Add the peanut oil and turn the heat to low. Add the Pickled Ginger and sauté for 1 minute. Turn off the heat. Add the vinegar and sugar. Turn the heat to low and stir until the sugar dissolves. Add the scallions and coriander. Stir for 30 seconds. Turn off the heat. Add the Chili Oil and sesame oil. Pour the sauce over the cabbage and toss well. Serve at room temperature or slightly chilled.

Stored in the refrigerator, Chinese Coleslaw will last several days.

SERVES 8 to 10

Beet and Water Chestnut Salad

I used to worry about people not liking beets. This recipe dispelled that fear.

I have gotten a lot of mileage out of this strikingly colorful salad. The deep red, almost burgundy beet rounds accented with the snow-white water chestnuts on a bed of green watercress attracts the diner's eye immediately. I frequently serve this for large buffet dinners.

4 bunches (about 16 small) beets (see step 1)
1 cup fresh water chestnuts, peeled and cut into ¼-inch circles

DRESSING
2 tablespoons red wine vinegar
2 tablespoons Chinese black vinegar
2 tablespoons Japanese rice vinegar
2 tablespoons Chinese red vinegar
½ teaspoon salt
4 teaspoons Dijon mustard
1 teaspoon minced garlic
3 tablespoons corn oil
6 tablespoons olive oil
¼ cup chopped scallions, white and green parts included
   Freshly ground black pepper (15 turns of the mill)

1 bunch watercress, 2-inches of stems removed

GARNISH
1 whole scallion, cut into ⅛-inch rounds
1 tablespoon chopped parsley

1. While the beets are still tied, cut the stems, leaving 3 inches attached to the beet. The purpose of this is so that the beets won't bleed when steamed. Wash the beets thoroughly, then

steam them for about 20 minutes or until they are cooked through. The steaming time will depend on the size of the beets. Remove and discard the stems and skin. Cut the beets into ¼-inch circles. The yield should be 2½ cups. Place the beets in a bowl. Place the water chestnuts in a separate bowl.

2. Make the dressing by mixing together the 4 vinegars, salt, and mustard. Stir until the salt is dissolved, then add the garlic, corn oil, olive oil, scallions, and pepper. Mix until the dressing has thickened slightly. The yield should be 1 cup.

3. Mix ¾ cup of the dressing with the beets and ¼ cup with the water chestnuts. Marinate both for 1 hour.

4. Place the watercress on a white serving platter. Arrange the beets in a circle on top of the watercress, then place the water chestnuts in the center of the circle. Garnish with chopped scallions and parsley. Serve at room temperature.

Peel the beets while they are still warm; that way the skin comes off much more easily.

Red wine vinegar is made from grapes. Chinese black vinegar is made from rice and soy sauce. Chinese red vinegar is made from malt, rice, and salt. Japanese rice vinegar is made from rice.

As a substitute for the water chestnuts you can use jicama, which is a Mexican radish. It is a large, round irregular shape. Peel and then slice it into large rounds, ⅜-inch thick, then pile the rounds on top of each other and quarter. Trim each piece into a round so as to simulate a round water chestnut.

This salad can be prepared early in the day through step 2.

SERVES 8

String Bean Salad with
Double Sesame Dressing

I like to serve this salad as a room-temperature vegetable dish to round out the menu for a small dinner party or a buffet. This same dressing works well on cauliflower or asparagus.

1 tablespoon unhulled sesame seeds

1½ pounds string beans

DOUBLE SESAME DRESSING
3 tablespoons red wine vinegar
3 tablespoons light soy sauce
2 teaspoons Spicy Mustard Sauce (see page 14)
2 teaspoons sugar
3 tablespoons Oriental sesame oil
1 teaspoon minced garlic
¼ cup finely chopped scallions, white and green parts
   included
¼ cup finely chopped red sweet peppers
¼ cup finely chopped yellow Holland peppers

1. Place a wok over high heat for about 1 minute or until it smokes. Add the sesame seeds. Turn the heat to low and dry-cook them for 3 to 5 minutes or until they brown. Empty the sesame seeds onto a flat plate.

2. Steam the string beans 3 to 5 minutes or until they have softened but still have some crunch. Remove them from the steamer. To stop the cooking and hold the color, plunge the beans into a bowl of ice-cold water for about a minute or until they cool. Drain them in a colander set over a bowl. After the beans are dry, remove the stem ends.

3. Make the Double Sesame Dressing by mixing together the vinegar, soy sauce, Spicy Mustard Sauce, sugar, and sesame oil. Stir until the dressing has thickened slightly, then add the garlic, scallions, and red and yellow peppers. Mix until well combined.

4. Place the string beans in a large bowl and add the dressing. Toss well.

5. Sprinkle with sesame seeds. Serve on a flat white serving platter.

This salad can be prepared early in the day through step 3.

SERVES 8

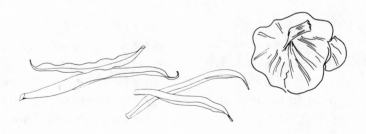

Long Bean, Roasted Pepper, and Goat Cheese Salad

If you asked me what I wanted for lunch, I would say this salad. It is yet another by-product of the master recipe for Hunan Roasted Peppers. If you don't have time to make that recipe, then just roast 1 yellow and 1 red pepper according to the procedure on page 25 and use that as a substitute.

½ recipe Hunan Roasted Peppers (see page 129)

½ pound Chinese long beans
¼ cup unhulled sesame seeds
One 7-ounce cylinder goat cheese

DRESSING
1½ tablespoons Chinese red vinegar
½ teaspoon salt
¾ teaspoon Dijon mustard
¾ teaspoon minced garlic
3 tablespoons corn oil
1½ tablespoons olive oil
Freshly ground black pepper (10 turns of the mill)

SPECIAL EQUIPMENT
Unwaxed dental floss

1. Make the Hunan Roasted Peppers.
2. Steam the long beans for 3 to 4 minutes or until they have softened but still have some crunch. Remove them from the steamer. Plunge the beans into a bowl of ice-cold water for about a minute or until they cool. Drain them in a colander set over a bowl. After the beans are dry, remove the stem ends.

3. Place a wok over high heat for about 1 minute or until it smokes. Add the sesame seeds. Turn the heat to low and dry-cook them for 3 to 5 minutes or until they brown. Empty the sesame seeds onto a flat plate.

4. Using dental floss, cut the goat cheese into 4 or 5 equal rounds. Dip the rounds into the sesame seeds, coating them on both sides.

5. Make the dressing by mixing together the vinegar, salt, and mustard. Stir until the salt is dissolved; then add the garlic, corn oil, olive oil, and black pepper. Continue to mix until the dressing has thickened slightly.

6. Choose a flat serving dish, preferably white. Arrange the long beans to form a border. Scatter the roasted peppers on top of the beans. Place the sesame-coated cheese rounds in an overlapping pattern in the center of the serving dish. Spoon the dressing over the long beans and peppers. Serve at room temperature.

For the Chinese long beans you can substitute American string beans or French haricots verts.

Long Bean, Roasted Pepper, and Goat Cheese Salad can be prepared early in the day through step 5.

SERVES 4 to 5

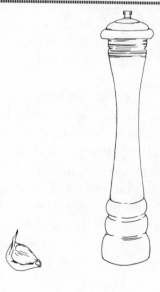

Jicama and Dandelion Salad

Jicama is a large brown Mexican radish. When it is peeled, it is white underneath. At its best, it is sweet and crunchy and works beautifully in salads. When it turns old, it becomes starchy and loses its sweet taste. Like water chestnuts, jicama should feel hard and have no visible trace of mold.

6 slices bacon, diced

DRESSING
3 tablespoons Chinese red vinegar
1½ teaspoons salt
1½ teaspoons Dijon mustard
1½ teaspoons minced garlic
1 teaspoon Hot Sauce (see pp. 10–11)
6 tablespoons corn oil
3 tablespoons olive oil

1 medium-large jicama, peeled, rinsed, and cut into thick, long strips (about 6 cups)
1 bunch dandelion greens (4 cups after stems removed)
½ cup diced sweet peppers (combination of red and yellow)
⅓ cup snipped chives

1. Fry the diced bacon until crisp. Drain on paper towels.

2. Make the dressing by mixing together the vinegar, salt, and mustard. Stir until the salt is dissolved; then add the garlic, Hot Sauce, corn oil, and olive oil. Continue to mix until the dressing has thickened slightly.

3. Place the jicama in a large bowl. Add the dressing. Toss the jicama with the dressing for about 1 minute. Add the dandelion greens, red and yellow peppers, chives, and bacon. Continue to toss until all the ingredients have been well combined with the dressing. Serve immediately.

For the dandelion greens you can substitute watercress.

This salad can be prepared early in the day through step 2.

SERVES 6

Celery Root, Snow Pea, and Radicchio Salad

  1 pound celery root, peeled and shredded (about 4 cups)
1½ teaspoons salt
  2 teaspoons lemon juice

DRESSING
  3 tablespoons Chinese red vinegar
 ½ teaspoon salt
1½ tablespoons Dijon mustard
1½ teaspoons minced garlic
  6 tablespoons corn oil
  3 tablespoons olive oil
  3 tablespoons sliced (⅛-inch rounds) scallion, white and green parts included
  3 tablespoons parsley
  Freshly ground black pepper (15 turns of the mill)

  1 small head radicchio, halved and shredded (about 2½ cups)
1½ cups snow peas, strung and shredded

1. Toss the celery root in the salt and lemon juice. Allow to stand for 1 hour. Rinse the celery root in cold water; drain and dry it thoroughly on paper towels.

2. Make the dressing by mixing together the vinegar, salt, and mustard. Stir until the salt is dissolved; then add the garlic, corn oil, olive oil, scallions, parsley, and pepper. Mix until the dressing has thickened slightly.

3. Place the celery root, radicchio, and snow peas in a large bowl. Add the dressing and toss well. Serve within the hour on a flat white serving dish.

This salad can be prepared early in the day through step 2.

SERVES 8

Spring Ginger Crab Salad

This mayonnaise-based dressing has the enticing Oriental influence of Pickled Ginger and Spicy Mustard Sauce combined with the sweetness of Italian balsamic vinegar. It is also very special on steamed lobster, shrimp, or chicken.

1 pound lump crabmeat

DRESSING
¾ cup mayonnaise
1 tablespoon Spicy Mustard Sauce (see page 14)
1 teaspoon balsamic vinegar
  Freshly ground white pepper (20 turns of the mill)
½ cup finely chopped scallions, white and green parts
    included
¼ cup Pickled Ginger (see pp. 134–135)

GARNISH
1 small head radicchio, shredded
3 tablespoons chopped coriander leaves

1. Pick over the crabmeat carefully to remove any traces of cartilage or shell.
2. Make the dressing by mixing together the mayonnaise, Spicy Mustard Sauce, vinegar, pepper, scallions, and Pickled Ginger. Add the crabmeat and toss until well combined.
3. Arrange the radicchio to cover a flat serving platter. Place the crab salad in the center, leaving a 2-inch border of radicchio. Sprinkle with coriander and serve slightly chilled.

For the radicchio you can substitute arugula or watercress.

If you are making the crab salad early in the day, remove it from the refrigerator 30 minutes before serving.

SERVES 4

Barbecued Roast Duck Salad

There are certain dishes that are reserved for people you love—or someone who is offering you a contract with lots of zeros. Barbecued Roast Duck Salad is one of them, and worth every bit of the effort.

1 Barbecued Roast Duck, freshly roasted, at room temperature (see pp. 236–239)

DRESSING
6 tablespoons corn oil
2 tablespoons Chinese red vinegar
2 teaspoons Dijon mustard
1 tablespoon finely shredded Pickled Ginger (see pp. 134–135)
  Freshly ground black pepper (10 turns of the mill)
1 tablespoon chopped parsley
1 tablespoon chopped dill

1 bunch arugula
1 small Belgian endive, split and cut into strips
1 whole scallion, shredded
¾ cup shredded sweet peppers (combination of red and yellow)
½ ripe mango, cut into strips (approximately ½ cup)

1. *To Bone a Roast Duck:* Remove the wings and legs of the duck and reserve for another use, for instance, as an addition to Vegetable Fried Wild Rice (see pp. 97–99). Bone the duck breast, keeping the skin and meat intact. Remove the meat from the breast by beginning at the shoulder (wishbone) and making one long cut. Follow the upper ridge or contour of the breastbone. Repeat the procedure with the other side. You should now have two boned halves, meat and skin attached. Make ½-inch cross-cuts on both halves. Bone both thighs by removing the thigh meat and skin in one piece. Make ½-inch cross cuts on this meat.

2. Make the dressing by mixing together the corn oil, vinegar, and mustard. Stir until the mixture thickens. Add the Pickled Ginger, pepper, parsley, and dill, stirring until well combined.

3. While the arugula is still tied, cut off and discard 2 inches of the stem. Wash the arugula, then spin-dry. Place a bed of arugula on a flat (preferably white) serving platter.

4. Arrange the endive, scallion, sweet peppers, and mango around the arugula, forming a border. Remix the dressing and spoon it over the salad. Place the duck breast and thighs in the center, arranged to look like a whole duck breast and thighs flattened out. Serve immediately.

Save the extra pieces of meat to add to fried rice or Spinach Lo Mein.

When you are roasting the duck to use in this salad, you will not need the defatted drippings from the bottom of the roasting pan nor the sauce that is made from the drippings. Make the sauce anyway, then freeze it and use in the seasoning sauce for Spinach Lo Mein or Miniature Vegetables with Shallots and Cremini Mushrooms.

When mangos are not around, try substituting a ripe pear or a crisp apple. The acidity of the fruit is necessary to offset the richness of the duck.

The duck can be roasted several hours in advance. You can also make the dressing several hours ahead. But the final assembling of the salad must be done at the last minute.

SERVES 2 to 4

Sichuan Chicken Salad

This is an updated version of a chicken salad I learned from Madame Chu, who was the first person to teach Chinese cooking in America. It makes a great lunch anytime of the year. I also frequently include it as a room-temperature dish when preparing a buffet dinner.

1 medium-size leek
2 whole chicken breasts (totaling 1½ pounds)
2 cups shredded Chinese Napa cabbage
2 cups shredded Belgian endive

DRESSING
⅓ cup sliced (⅛-inch rounds) scallions, white and green
    parts included
¼ cup diced red sweet pepper
¼ cup diced yellow Holland pepper
2 teaspoons minced garlic
2 teaspoons minced ginger
1 tablespoon dark soy sauce
1 tablespoon hoisin sauce
2 teaspoons honey
1 teaspoon Hot Sauce (see pp. 10–11)
1 teaspoon Sichuan Peppercorn Powder (see page 13)
1 tablespoon peanut oil
1 tablespoon Oriental sesame oil

2 cups peanut oil for deep-frying

GARNISH
2 to 3 ounces rice noodles

1. Remove the root end of the leek, then split the leek in half lengthwise all the way through. Place it under running warm water to remove all traces of sand. Cut the green part only into 3-inch pieces (reserve the white part for use in other recipes).

2. In a 2-quart saucepan with a tight-fitting cover, bring 2 inches of water to a rolling boil. Add the chicken breasts. Place the leeks on top. Cover, turn the heat to low, and simmer 20 minutes or until the chicken breasts are cooked all the way through. Remove the chicken breasts from the saucepan and allow them to drain. Reserve the chicken stock for another use. Remove the skin, then allow the chicken to cool. Shred the chicken breasts by tearing the meat into strips with your fingers.

3. Combine the chicken, cabbage, and endive in a large bowl.

4. In one bowl, combine scallions, red and yellow peppers, garlic, and ginger. In another bowl, combine the soy sauce, hoisin sauce, honey, Hot Sauce, and Sichuan Peppercorn Powder.

5. Place a wok over high heat for about 1 minute or until it smokes. Add 1 tablespoon peanut oil and heat until it is hot but not smoking. Add the scallion and peppers mixture. Stir over high heat for about 1 minute. Add the soy and hoisin sauce mixture, stirring well for 30 seconds. Turn off the heat. Add the sesame oil. Pour the dressing into the bowl over the chicken, endive, and cabbage. Toss until well combined.

6. Place a wok over high heat. Add 2 cups peanut oil and heat until the oil reaches 375°. Add a loose handful of rice noodles to the oil and fry for about 3 seconds or until the rice noodles puff up but before they turn brown. Remove them from the wok with a wire strainer and drain on paper towels. Repeat the procedure with a few more handfuls, deep-frying one handful at a time.

7. Arrange the rice noodles around the edges of a flat serving dish to form a border. Place the chicken salad in the center. Serve at room temperature.

The entire preparation can be done early in the day, leaving only the tossing of the chicken with the sauce to the last minute.

SERVES 3 to 4

Scallop Salad

  1 pound small bay scallops
  5 tablespoons fresh lime juice
  ¼ cup sour cream
  1 teaspoon Japanese rice vinegar
  ½ teaspoon sugar
  ¼ cup finely shredded scallions, white and green parts
     included
  ¼ cup kirby cucumber, sliced thinly into rounds
  ½ teaspoon salt
     Freshly ground white pepper (10 turns of the mill)
  2 ounces fresh salmon caviar
  2 cups shredded Chinese Napa cabbage

  GARNISH
  2 tablespoons shredded Pickled Ginger (see pp. 134–135)

1. Rinse the scallops, then drain and dry them thoroughly. If they are big, slice them in half. Place the scallops in a bowl, add the lime juice, and stir well to coat. Cover the bowl and allow the scallops to marinate in the refrigerator for 12 hours.

2. In another bowl combine the sour cream, rice vinegar, sugar, scallions, cucumbers, salt, and pepper. Fold in the caviar.

3. Drain the scallops from the marinade and fold them into the sour cream mixture.

4. Place the cabbage on a flat, white serving dish. Place the scallop mixture on top of the cabbage and garnish with ginger shreds. Serve slightly chilled.

Scallop Salad can be prepared early in the day through step 2.

SERVES 8

Soups

YELLOW SPLIT PEA AND CORIANDER SOUP

CHICKEN STOCK

REDUCED CHICKEN STOCK

CHINESE BOUILLABAISSE WITH
BLACK BEAN AIOLI

SPICY CELERY ROOT AND LEEK SOUP

CHICKEN VEGETABLE SOUP

CHINESE POT-AU-FEU

MUSHROOM BISQUE

PESTO WONTONS IN BRODO

MISO AND ESCAROLE SOUP

SHRIMP, SPINACH, AND ICICLE RADISH SOUP

Yellow Split Pea and Coriander Soup

With its fresh minced ginger and coriander leaves, Yellow Split Pea and Coriander Soup is an Eastern variation of a Swedish classic.

2 tablespoons sweet butter
2 teaspoons minced ginger
¼ cup chopped coriander leaves
1 cup yellow split peas, rinsed
4 cups Chicken Stock, preferably salt-free (see pp. 76–77)
Freshly ground black pepper (20 turns of the mill)
Salt to taste
1 tablespoon lemon juice

GARNISH
1 lemon, sliced into thin circles

1. Melt the butter in a heavy saucepan over low heat. Add the ginger and coriander; sauté for 2 to 3 minutes.

2. Add the split peas and chicken stock; stir, then bring to a simmer. Add the pepper and optional salt. Partially cover and continue to simmer for 40 minutes, stirring occasionally, until the peas soften but before they become pureed.

3. Turn off the heat, add the lemon juice, stir briefly. Portion out the soup into 4 bowls, placing a lemon slice in the center of each one. Serve piping hot.

Coriander is also known as cilantro or Chinese parsley.

SERVES 4

Chicken Stock

I rarely make chicken stock out of just chicken, and almost never buy a chicken to make stock. Instead I freeze roasted carcasses from chickens, ducks, and turkeys. They add great flavor to the stock. I also freeze raw carcasses from chickens and ducks that I bone; and I save parts that I am not using in a recipe, such as legs and giblets from Rock Cornish hens, turkey, and all types of poultry. (Raw poultry parts can be frozen for 6 months, but a cooked carcass can only be frozen for 1 month.) When I can't close my freezer, it's time to make stock.

1 chicken, weighing 4 to 5 pounds, cut into pieces (giblets and skin included, liver excluded)
4 cups leeks, green parts only, split and cut into 2-inch pieces
2 thin slices ginger
6 whole black peppercorns

1. Rinse the chicken pieces under cold running water, then place them in a large stockpot. Add enough water to cover the parts by 2 inches. Bring to a simmer over high heat. With a fine-mesh skimmer, remove the scum as it rises to the top. This skimming process will take about 10 minutes.

2. Add the leeks, ginger, and peppercorns to the stockpot. Turn the heat to low and simmer the stock uncovered for 6 to 8 hours, stirring occasionally.

3. Strain the stock through a colander and then through a fine-mesh sieve (or line a strainer with cheesecloth that has been rinsed under cold running water and then wrung out).

4. Refrigerate the stock uncovered until it has thoroughly cooled and the fat has solidified. It is very important to allow the stock to cool in the refrigerator without a cover to prevent it from becoming sour. Before using the stock, lift the layer of fat off the top.

5. Store in the refrigerator for up to 1 week (longer if it is brought to a simmer every day). Or freeze it in small glass jars filled two-thirds full, allowing space for expansion so that the glass won't break. Chicken Stock can also be frozen in ice cube trays, after which the frozen stock cubes can be placed in a glass jar or plastic bag.

VEAL STOCK VARIATION
In order to make veal stock, you may substitute veal scraps and bones weighing 4 to 5 pounds instead of the chicken. A good way to acquire these scraps and bones is to make Soong Stuffed Loin of Veal.

Larger or smaller quantities of stock can be made than called for in this sample recipe. When using less than 4 or 5 pounds of poultry parts, allow the water to cover the parts by at least 6 inches, since less liquid is involved and therefore will evaporate more rapidly. If the level of water becomes too shallow, add more water as necessary.

YIELDS 1 quart

Reduced Chicken Stock

When I want to enrich a sauce or soup, I add Reduced Chicken Stock as a substitute for glace de poulet *or demi-glace.*

2 quarts defatted and salt-free Chicken Stock (see pp. 76–77)

1. Place the stock in a saucepan and reduce over the lowest possible heat until 1 cup remains.
2. Pour small quantities of the reduced stock into lidded glass jars. Store in the refrigerator for 1 week or in the freezer up to 1 year.

For the chicken stock, you can substitute any type of defatted, salt-free stock, such as beef or veal.

Keep some frozen in small glass jars for quick defrosting.

YIELDS 1 cup

Chinese Bouillabaisse with
Black Bean Aioli

Aioli is a garlic mayonnaise traditionally served in a fish soup called Bouillabaisse, which originated in Marseilles, France. I have added the ancient Chinese spice called fermented black beans and also winter melon, which is a variety of Chinese squash. More than a soup, Bouillabaisse makes a wonderful dinner.

BLACK BEAN AIOLI
½ cup diced French bread without the crust
2 tablespoons red wine vinegar
3 large cloves garlic
2 egg yolks, at room temperature
2 teaspoons minced fermented black beans
¾ cup olive oil

BOUILLABAISSE
⅓ cup dried Chinese mushrooms
1 tablespoon reduced mushroom stock (see step 2)
6 cups Chicken Stock, preferably salt-free (see pp. 76–77)
¾ teaspoon saffron
1½ medium-size leeks
2 dozen Little Neck clams
2 tablespoons cornmeal
One 1-pound piece (a 1-inch wedge) winter melon (see step 6)
One 1¼-pound live lobster
½ pound scallops
½ pound medium shrimp in the shell (21–25 to the pound)
¼ cup Tomato Sauce (see pp. 16–17)
Freshly ground black pepper (10 turns of the mill)
1 tablespoon medium-dry sherry

12 small rounds French bread, toasted

1. In a mixing bowl, soak the ½ cup diced French bread with the vinegar for about 5 minutes. Mash it until it becomes a paste. Squeeze the paste, extracting and then discarding the excess vinegar (if any). Finely mince the garlic, then add it along with the egg yolks and black beans to the bread paste. Whisk the mixture while adding ¼ cup of the oil, drop by drop. When the mixture begins to thicken, drizzle in the remaining ½ cup oil. Continue to whisk until the mixture thickens to the consistency of a thick mayonnaise. Refrigerate if making early in the day.

2. Rinse the mushrooms under cold running water. In a small bowl, soak them in cold water to cover for about 1 hour or until soft. Squeeze them over the bowl. Remove the stems and dice the mushrooms. Set the mushrooms aside. Place the stems in a saucepan. Add the mushroom liquid. Reduce until about 1 tablespoon remains. Strain the mushroom stock. Discard the stems. Add the mushroom stock to the chicken stock.

3. Place this stock in a 3- to 4-quart casserole. Bring to a simmer. Add the saffron. Turn the heat off. Allow the stock to steep for 1 hour uncovered.

4. Remove the root ends of the leeks, then split the leeks in half lengthwise all the way through. Place them under forcefully running warm water to remove all traces of sand. Then dice the white and also the tender light green parts (reserve the dark green part for Tomato Sauce or stock). The yield should be 1½ cups diced leeks.

5. Scrub the clams under cold running water, then place them in a bowl filled with fresh water to which the cornmeal has been added. Allow the clams to soak for 30 minutes. Scrub the clams again under cold running water, then place them in a clean bowl.

6. Cut off the rind from the winter melon and discard. Cut in half lengthwise, then slice thin. The yield should be approximately 2 cups.

7. Using a heavy cleaver and rubber mallet, sever the spinal column of the lobster near the head almost all the way through. This will kill the lobster instantly. Chop the body of the lobster into 2-inch sections. Crack the claws. Remove the brain (the gelatinous substance in the top of the head).

Cut the tail in half lengthwise and remove the intestinal tract. Place the lobster in a bowl.

8. Rinse the scallops and shrimp, then drain.

9. Bring the stock to a simmer over high heat. Add the clams and cook over high heat until they open. (The clams will take between 1 and 7 minutes to open. The faster they do, the fresher they are.) Using a wire strainer or slotted spoon, remove the clams from the stock as they begin to open. Place them on a large enamel paella dish.

10. Add the mushrooms, leeks, and tomato sauce; simmer over low heat for 3 minutes. Add the lobster pieces and winter melon; simmer 3 minutes. Add the scallops and shrimp; simmer another 2 minutes. Add the pepper and sherry; continue to simmer another minute.

11. Pour the contents of the casserole over the clams and serve with toasted French bread and Black Bean Aioli. Each diner spreads some Black Bean Aioli on the toasted bread, then floats the bread in her own soupbowl.

Fermented black beans can be purchased in Chinese groceries and sometimes in American supermarkets. They can be stored indefinitely on the shelf or in the refrigerator in a lidded glass jar. If kept in the refrigerator, they will stay moister.

Zucchini or summer yellow squash can be substituted for the winter melon.

This soup can be prepared several hours in advance through step 10 if you cut off one minute of cooking time from the lobster, scallops and shrimp, and then separate the shellfish from the soup. By doing this, the shellfish will not be overcooked when you rewarm the soup.

SERVES 4 to 6

Spicy Celery Root and Leek Soup

Autumn is the height of the celery root season, an excellent time to make this sweet, sour, salty, spicy soup.

Try to choose a medium-size celery root (about 1 pound), because larger ones are sometimes pithy.

1 medium-size leek
1 tablespoon sweet butter
4 cups Chicken Stock (see pp. 76–77)
2 cups celery root, cut into julienne
1 cup chopped, seeded, well-ripened tomatoes
1 tablespoon dark soy sauce
1 tablespoon Chinese red vinegar
½ teaspoon salt
½ teaspoon Hot Sauce (see pp. 10–11)
½ teaspoon sugar

1. Remove the root end of the leek, then split the leek in half lengthwise all the way through. Place it under forcefully running warm water to remove all traces of sand. Then cut the white and also the tender light green parts into ⅛-inch half circles (reserve the dark green part for Tomato Sauce or stock). The yield should be 1 cup thinly sliced leeks.

2. In a 1½- to 2-quart saucepan, heat the butter until it foams. Add the leeks and sauté over low heat for about 5 minutes. Add the chicken stock. Turn the heat to high and bring the stock to a simmer. Add the celery root and tomatoes. Simmer the soup without a cover for about 5 minutes.

3. Add the soy sauce, vinegar, salt, Hot Sauce, and sugar. Continue to simmer another minute or two. Serve piping hot.

This soup can be prepared early in the day.

SERVES 4 to 6

Chicken Vegetable Soup

This soup only takes a few minutes to put together. It is also low in calories, nutritious, and tastes delicious.

4 cups Chicken Stock (see pp. 76–77)
1 tablespoon oyster sauce
1 tablespoon dark soy sauce
½ pound diced boneless, skinless chicken
2 thin slices ginger
1 cup snow peas, strung and left whole
2 cups slant-cut (1½-inch thick) bok choy, white and green
    parts included
⅓ cup sliced (⅛-inch rounds) scallions, white and green
    parts included
Freshly ground white pepper (20 turns of the mill)

1. Bring the chicken stock, oyster sauce, and soy sauce to a simmer in a 1½- to 2-quart saucepan.
2. Add the chicken and simmer 1 minute.
3. Add the ginger slices, snow peas, bok choy, scallions, and pepper. Simmer uncovered for 3 minutes. Remove the ginger. Serve piping hot.

As a substitute for the oyster sauce and dark soy sauce, you can use ¼ cup vegetable drippings from Shanghai Vegetarian Spring Rolls or ¼ cup of the defatted sauce from Barbecued Roast Duck.

A nice addition to this soup is leftover Scallion Ginger Crepes, shredded and added at the last minute.

This soup can be prepared early in the day through step 2.

SERVES 4 to 6

Chinese Pot-au-feu

An entrée soup that provides soup, meat, and vegetables in one dish, Chinese Pot-au-feu is a perfect winter menu selection for a family-style or informal dinner. It has an intense broth, resulting from the slow simmering of the beef, chicken, and pork.

8 cups Chicken Stock, preferably salt-free (see pp. 76–77)
1 small flank steak, trimmed
½ pound boneless pork, such as butt
10 whole black peppercorns
2 teaspoons salt
1 carrot
1 large Spanish onion, peeled, and halved
  Few sprigs parsley
2 stalks celery, with leaves
1 chicken, weighing 4 pounds
2 medium-size leeks
3 cups thickly shredded bok choy, white and green parts
  included
2 cups snow peas, strung and left whole

CREAMY MUSTARD SAUCE
¼ cup Spicy Mustard Sauce (see page 14)
¼ cup heavy cream

1. In a large, 8-quart enamel casserole, bring the chicken stock to a simmer. Add the flank steak, pork, peppercorns, salt, carrot, onion, parsley, and celery. Cover loosely and simmer over low heat for 2 hours.

2. Rinse the chicken and drain. Place the whole chicken in the casserole and continue to simmer covered for another 1¼ to 1½ hours.

3. Remove the flank steak, pork, and chicken from the casserole to a serving platter. Strain the stock, then remove the fat.

Return the strained, defatted stock to the casserole and bring the stock to a simmer.

4. Remove the root ends of the leeks, then split the leeks in half lengthwise all the way through. Place them under forcefully running warm water to remove all traces of sand. Then cut the white and also the tender light green parts into ⅛-inch half circles (reserve the dark green part for Tomato Sauce or stock). The yield should be 2 cups cut leeks. Add the leeks to the simmering stock and cook for 10 minutes uncovered over low heat.

5. Add the bok choy and simmer 1 minute, then add the snow peas, continuing to simmer another minute.

6. While the pot-au-feu is simmering, make the Creamy Mustard Sauce by mixing together the Spicy Mustard Sauce and cream in a small serving bowl. Stir until well combined.

7. Slice the flank steak in half lengthwise with the grain, then cut the steak against the grain into thin slices. Also cut the pork into thin slices. Using a poultry shears, cut the chicken into small serving pieces. Arrange the steak and pork slices, along with the chicken pieces, on the platter. Moisten them with ½ cup of the stock.

8. Remove the soup from the casserole to a soup tureen, then bring it to the table, along with the platter of meat and the Creamy Mustard Sauce. Serve each individual a ladleful of piping-hot soup in a large soup or pasta bowl. Each diner helps herself to the meat platter, adding the meats, along with a teaspoon of Creamy Mustard Sauce, to the soup.

This soup can be prepared ahead through step 4.

SERVES 6 to 8

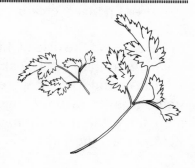

Mushroom Bisque

Shiitake mushrooms are sold both fresh and dried in America. They have become so popular in their fresh state that they are grown on both coasts. When sold dried, they are packaged under various names including black mushrooms, black forest mushrooms, shiitake, or just dried mushrooms from Japan. Dried Chinese mushrooms are a close relative to shiitake. They have a memorably rich flavor. All dried mushrooms have a more intense flavor than their fresh counterparts as a result of the drying process.

Since the stems of dried Chinese mushrooms are too hard to be eaten, and since the stems of fresh shiitake are usually too woody to be eaten, they can be boiled in water to extract their flavor, resulting in a reduced mushroom stock. I call this glace de champignon. *Always reduce, strain, and save mushroom stock from any dried mushrooms. I consider this culinary gold and it is a culinary crime to throw it away.*

¾ cup dried Chinese mushrooms
2 cups fresh shiitake mushrooms
¼ cup reduced mushroom stock (see step 1)
4 tablespoons sweet butter
1½ tablespoons dark soy sauce
2 cups veal stock, preferably salt-free (see page 77)
¼ cup port
Freshly ground black pepper (20 turns of the mill)
¼ cup heavy cream

1. Rinse the dried Chinese mushrooms under cold running water. In a small bowl, soak them in cold water to cover for about 1 hour or until soft. Squeeze them over the bowl. Remove the stems from both the Chinese and the shiitake mushrooms and then shred the mushrooms. Set the mushrooms aside. Place the stems in a saucepan. Add the mushroom liquid. Reduce until

about ¼ cup remains. Strain the mushroom stock and reserve. Discard the stems.

2. In a 3-quart saucepan, heat the butter over low heat until it melts. Add the shiitake and the Chinese mushrooms. Sauté for 3 minutes. Add the soy sauce and sauté another 5 minutes. Turn the heat to high and add the veal stock and the mushroom stock. When the stock comes to a simmer, turn the heat to low. Simmer another few minutes.

3. In a separate saucepan, boil the port until it has reduced to about 3 tablespoons. If the port self-ignites, allow the flame to burn out. Add the port to the soup along with the pepper and the cream. Continue to simmer another minute over low heat. Serve piping hot.

This soup can be prepared early in the day.

You can substitute chicken stock for the veal stock.

SERVES 4 to 6

Pesto Wontons in Brodo

A classic Italian dish is Pasta in Brodo, brodo *being the basic stock used. The wontons in this recipe are served in the stock the way Italians would serve tortellini or another stuffed pasta.*

FILLING
   1 cup ricotta cheese
2½ cups basil leaves
   ¼ cup olive oil
   ¼ cup pine nuts
   ½ cup freshly grated Parmesan cheese
   1 teaspoon salt
     Freshly ground black pepper (20 turns of the mill)

50 thin square wonton wrappers
   1 teaspoon salt

   4 cups Chicken Stock (see pp. 76–77)
   2 whole scallions, shredded
   1 cup shredded bok choy, white and green parts included

1. Place the ricotta in a strainer set over a bowl in the refrigerator and allow it to drain at least 12 hours.

2. Wash and spin-dry the basil leaves. Place the basil leaves and oil in the bowl of a food processor. Process until the mixture is finely chopped. Remove the mixture from the bowl of the food processor and measure out ¼ cup. Place the leftover basil mixture in a lidded glass jar. Store it in the refrigerator for up to 2 weeks or in the freezer for several months.

3. Make the filling by placing the drained ricotta in a bowl along with the ¼ cup basil mixture, pine nuts, Parmesan cheese, 1 teaspoon salt, and pepper. Stir well to combine the ingredients.

4. Bring a kettle of water to a rolling boil.

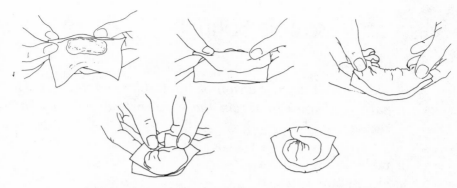

5. *To Make the Wontons* Place 1 teaspoon of filling in the lower center of a wonton wrapper. Moisten the edge farthest from you with water. Fold the unmoistened edge over the filling, away from you, and up to the moistened edge. Seal the 2 edges together. Make a ¼-inch crease upward, on the sealed edge, turning the edge up. With the thumb and index finger of both hands, take the corners nearest you and pull them together. The corners away from you should be pointing straight up; the corners nearest you should lie flat. Moisten one of the near corners and place it on top of the other corner, sealing them together. The result should resemble a nun's hat. Cover the wontons with a damp cloth until ready to poach.

6. Add 1 teaspoon salt to the kettle of boiling water. Drop 5 wontons into the water, either by hand or with a wire strainer. Simmer the wontons gently for about 1 to 1½ minutes. Remove them with a wire strainer. Repeat the procedure, cooking 5 wontons at a time, until all have been poached.

7. While the wontons are cooking, heat the chicken stock until it simmers. Add the scallions and bok choy. Simmer 1 minute.

8. Place 4 to 6 wontons in each of 8 individual soup bowls. Spoon the broth, followed by a few shreds of bok choy and scallion, over the pesto wontons. Serve piping hot.

You can prepare the pesto wontons several hours in advance through step 5, provided that you refrigerate them.

SERVES 8 to 10

Miso and Escarole Soup

This is an Eastern version of the Italian escarole soup. I have used miso to season the soup instead of Parmesan cheese.

   2 tablespoons dark miso
   1 tablespoon water
   1 tablespoon sweet butter
1½ cups chopped Spanish onion
   1 tablespoon minced Pickled Ginger (see pp. 134–135)
   4 cups Chicken Stock, preferably salt-free (see pp. 76–77)
   ½ cup sliced carrots, in rounds
   ½ pound escarole, cut into 1-inch pieces
   1 cake fresh bean curd (3 ounces), thinly sliced into 1-inch pieces
   1 tablespoon dark soy sauce
   1 tablespoon lemon juice

1. Thin the miso by adding the water to it and mixing well.

2. In a 2½-quart saucepan, sauté the onions in the butter for about 5 minutes or until they brown. Add the Pickled Ginger and stir briefly.

3. Add the chicken stock, bring to a simmer. Turn the heat to low. Add the carrots; simmer 2 minutes. Add the escarole and simmer another 4 minutes. Add the bean curd and soy sauce. Simmer the soup another minute. Turn off the heat.

4. Add the miso and lemon juice. Cover and let sit 1 minute. Stir gently with a wooden spoon. Serve the soup piping hot.

Miso is a condiment composed of fermented soybeans, rice (or barley), and salt. It is sold in plastic bags, and once purchased it can be stored in the refrigerator for 1 year in a lidded glass jar.

SERVES 4 to 6

Shrimp, Spinach, and Icicle Radish Soup

2 cups Chicken Stock (see pp. 76–77)
2 cups fish stock
¼ pound small shrimp
2 tablespoons sweet butter
3 tablespoons minced shallots
1 cup shredded icicle radish
2 tablespoons shredded Pickled Ginger (see pp. 134–135)
¾ pound fresh spinach, stems removed, washed and
      spun-dry
   Freshly ground black pepper (10 turns of the mill)

1. Bring the chicken stock and fish stock to a simmer in a 1½-quart saucepan, uncovered.

2. Rinse the shrimp under cold running water and drain. Place the shrimp in the simmering soup for about 1 minute or until the shells turn pink. Turn off the heat. Using a slotted spoon, remove the shrimp from the saucepan and allow them to cool. When they have cooled, remove the shells, devein, and cut each shrimp into 4 pieces crosswise.

3. In a 2½- to 3-quart saucepan, heat the butter until it foams. Add the shallots and sauté over low heat for 2 minutes or until they begin to soften. Pour in the chicken and fish stock; bring to a simmer. Add the icicle radish and Pickled Ginger; continue to simmer another 3 minutes without a cover. Add the spinach; simmer 1 more minute. Add the pepper along with the cooked shrimp and simmer another 30 seconds. Serve in individual soup bowls.

If you don't have fish stock on hand, you can substitute bottled clam broth.

SERVES 4 to 6

Rice, Noodles, and Bread

BOILED KOKUHO ROSE RICE

VEGETABLE FRIED WILD RICE

CHINESE VEGETABLE RISOTTO

PASTA WITH SCALLOPS AND MISO

SPINACH LO MEIN

PASTA WITH FRESH WILD MUSHROOMS

LINGUINI WITH SEAFOOD CORIANDER SAUCE

RICE NOODLES PRIMAVERA

PASTA WITH EGGPLANT AND
OYSTER MUSHROOMS

CHINESE ROASTED PEPPER PASTA

LINGUINI WITH CHINESE RATATOUILLE

GRILLED VEGETABLE PASTA

SICHUAN PEPPERCORN LINGUINI

SCALLION GINGER CREPES

CHINESE HERO

CANDIED WALNUT AND SCALLION BREAD

CANDIED WALNUTS

Boiled Kokuho Rose Rice

When someone greets you in China, they say a phrase that is literally translated as "Have you eaten rice?" This is because if you have eaten rice, then you have really eaten, for in many parts of China rice comprises 80 percent of the peasants' diet. A typical day in the life of a Chinese worker would be to jump on his bike, peddle one and a half hours to work, do eight hours of hand irrigation in the fields, and then ride home. His dinner would consist of several bowls of rice, and the other food would be there to "season" it.

This basic rice recipe is for a very special rice called Kokuho Rose. It is a short-grain Japanese white rice that contains no talcum powder, as do many long-grain varieties. The purpose of the talcum powder is to keep the grains separate. Without the talcum, this rice is stickier than other varieties, but by using a one-to-one proportion of rice to water and by allowing the rice to relax, I am pleased with the texture and certainly the taste. I also like the challenge of cooking without chemicals, a challenge that becomes increasingly difficult in the twentieth century.

1 cup water
1 cup Kokuho Rose rice

1. Bring the water to a rapid boil over high heat in a heavy 1-quart enamel or stainless steel saucepan with a tight-fitting cover.

2. Place the rice in a strainer and rinse under cold running water. Drain.

3. Add the rice to the saucepan. When the water returns to a rapid boil, stir the rice with chopsticks in a figure-8 motion. Cover, reduce the heat to the lowest possible setting, and simmer the rice for 15 minutes. Turn off the heat and let the rice relax for 20 minutes. Do not remove the saucepan from the burner unless

you are cooking on an electric range. Remove the cover and stir the rice with chopsticks. Serve immediately.

For the Kokuho Rose rice, you can substitute any short-grain rice or you can substitute long-grain rice, in which case increase the water to 1¼ cups.

The rice will stay warm up to 30 minutes after the relaxing period if kept on the same gas burner.

If you wish to make the rice in advance, it can be rewarmed in a water bath, either on top of the range or in a preheated 350° oven.

Perfectly cooked rice has "fish eyes," or little holes that form on the top.

Leftover cooked rice can be used for fried rice, Chinese Crab Cakes, or Pine Nut Rice Stuffed Tomatoes.

SERVES 2 to 3

Vegetable Fried Wild Rice

The Chinese don't have wild rice, but that's no reason why we can't use it in preparing a Chinese dish. This version of fried rice goes with almost any kind of roasted or broiled fish, poultry, or meat.

1½ cups raw wild rice
3 cups Chicken Stock, preferably salt-free (see pp. 76–77)
1 cup mung bean sprouts
2 medium-size leeks

SEASONING SAUCE
2 tablespoons dark soy sauce
2 tablespoons oyster sauce

2 eggs
⅓ cup peanut oil
1 cup diced sweet peppers (combination of red and yellow)
1 cup strung and diced snow peas

1. Place the wild rice in a strainer. Rinse under cold running water then drain. Place the rice in a 3-quart saucepan with a tight-fitting cover. Add the chicken stock. Bring to a rapid boil over high heat. Stir with chopsticks, then turn the heat to low. Cover and simmer for 45 minutes to 1 hour or until the rice has absorbed the stock. Turn off the heat and allow the rice to relax for 30 minutes. If you're using an electric stove, remove the rice from the burner. The rice will yield 6 cups when cooked.

2. Place the bean sprouts on paper towels to dry.

3. Remove the root ends of the leeks, then split the leeks in half lengthwise all the way through. Place them under forcefully running warm water to remove all traces of sand. Then dice the white and also the tender light green parts (reserve the dark green part for Tomato Sauce or stock). The yield should be 2 cups diced leeks.

4. Make the seasoning sauce by combining the soy sauce and oyster sauce in a small bowl.

5. Beat the eggs in a bowl. Place a 12-inch cast-iron skillet over high heat for about 1 minute or until it smokes. Add 1 tablespoon of the peanut oil. While the oil is heating, rotate the skillet above the heat so that the oil is evenly distributed. Pour off the excess oil. Add the eggs all at once. Rotate the skillet so that a large, thin pancake is formed. When it has set, remove the egg pancake by inverting the skillet over a flat surface. Allow the pancake to cook, then dice.

6. Place a wok over high heat for about 1 minute or until it smokes. Add the bean sprouts. Allow them to scorch on one side for approximately 30 seconds, shaking the wok occasionally. Flip the bean sprouts in the wok and scorch them on the other side for another 30 seconds. Turn off the heat. Remove the bean sprouts to a plate.

7. Return the wok to high heat. Add 1½ tablespoons of the peanut oil. Add the leeks and stir-fry 2 to 3 minutes or until they have softened. If the leeks begin to scorch, turn the heat to medium. Add the red and yellow peppers; stir-fry 1 minute. Add the snow peas; stir-fry 30 seconds. Remove the vegetables from the wok.

8. Return the wok to high heat. Add the remaining peanut oil and the rice. Stir-fry 2 minutes or until the rice is hot and is coated with the oil. Add the seasoning sauce and continue to stir-fry another minute or until the rice has evenly absorbed the seasoning. Return the cooked vegetables to the wok, along with the diced egg pancake. Stir briefly to distribute the vegetables evenly. Empty the contents of the wok into a serving dish and serve hot or at room temperature.

Because it can be served at room temperature, you can prepare the dish several hours in advance.

A nice addition to this recipe would be the skin and meat from the wings and legs of Barbecued Roast Duck or Barbecued Roast Duck Salad.

SERVES 12 to 14

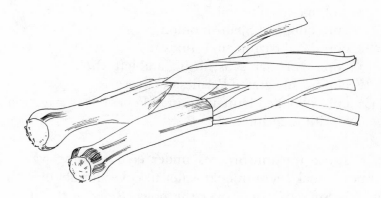

Chinese Vegetable Risotto

It is hard to think of what this rice dish does not go well with. Serve it with veal chops, roast chicken or duck, fish entrées, and more.

¼ cup dried Chinese mushrooms
1 tablespoon reduced mushroom stock (see step 1)
2½ cups Chicken Stock (see pp. 76–77)
1½ cups raw short-grain Italian rice (arborio)
1 teaspoon salt (if using salt-free chicken stock)
3 tablespoons olive oil
2 cups chopped Spanish onion
½ cup sliced carrots, in rounds
1 cup sugar snap peas, strung and left whole
½ cup freshly grated Parmesan cheese
1½ cups chopped Hunan Roasted Peppers (see page 129), with their juice

1. Rinse the mushrooms under cold running water. In a small bowl, soak them in cold water to cover for about 1 hour or until soft. Squeeze them over the bowl. Remove the stems and dice with mushrooms. Set the mushrooms aside. Place the stems in a saucepan. Add the mushroom liquid. Reduce until about 1 tablespoon remains. Strain the mushroom stock and reserve. Discard the stems.

2. Add the mushroom stock to the chicken stock.

3. Place the rice in a strainer. Rinse under cold running water, then drain. Place the rice and the chicken-mushroom stock in a 2-quart saucepan with a tight-fitting cover. Bring to a rapid boil over high heat. Add the optional salt. Stir with chopsticks, then turn the heat to low. Cover and simmer for 25 minutes or until the water has evaporated. Turn off the heat and allow the rice to relax about 30 minutes. If using an electric range, remove the saucepan from the heat source.

4. Heat 2 tablespoons of the olive oil in a wok or cast-iron skillet. Add the onions and sauté until they begin to brown. Add the carrots and mushrooms, continuing to cook another 2 minutes or until the carrots soften. Add the sugar snap peas and cook another minute. Turn off the heat.

5. Add the cooked rice to the skillet containing the vegetables. Sprinkle in the Parmesan cheese, then add the remaining 1 tablespoon olive oil.

6. Mix in the Hunan Roasted Peppers. Taste for seasoning and add more salt if necessary. Serve at room temperature.

Chinese Vegetable Risotto is best made several hours in advance and served at room temperature, but leftover portions can be refrigerated and brought to room temperature a day or two later.

As a substitute for the Hunan Roasted Peppers you can use a cup of leftover Chinese Ratatouille.

Arborio is the generic name of the most commonly imported variety of Italian rice. It is available under more than one brand name and can be obtained not only from Italian groceries but also from food shops and many department stores.

For the arborio rice you can substitute any short-grain rice, such as Kokuho Rose, and reduce the chicken stock to 1½ cups.

SERVES 12

Pasta with Scallops and Miso

This is a great pasta dish that uses a quick stir-fry and combines Oriental seasonings with Italian pasta.

⅓ pound scallops
Freshly ground black pepper (10 turns of the mill)

SEASONING SAUCE
2 tablespoons dark miso
1 tablespoon dark soy sauce
¼ cup Chicken Stock, preferably salt-free (see pp. 76–77)

½ pound fresh thin pasta
1 tablespoon sweet butter, melted
1 tablespoon peanut oil
1 tablespoon sweet butter
4 whole scallions, cut into ⅛-inch rounds
1 teaspoon minced garlic
2 teaspoons minced ginger
½ cup shredded fresh shiitake mushrooms
1 cup well-ripened tomatoes, cut into large dice

1. Rinse the scallops; drain, then dry on paper towels for 30 minutes. Change the paper towels several times. When the scallops are dry, sprinkle them with pepper.
2. Make the seasoning sauce by mixing together the miso, soy sauce, and chicken stock. Stir until well combined.
3. Preheat the oven to 250°.
4. Bring a large kettle of water to a rolling boil. Add the pasta and cook about 2 minutes. Drain in a colander, then toss the pasta with melted butter. Place the noodles on a flat serving dish. Keep them warm in the oven (without a cover).
5. Place a wok over high heat for about 1 minute or until it smokes. Add the peanut oil and heat for a few seconds, then add

the scallops and sauté about 2 minutes, allowing them to scorch on both sides. Remove them from the wok.

6. Turn the heat to low and add the 1 tablespoon butter. When it has melted, add the scallions, garlic, and ginger. Stir-fry about 30 seconds. Turn the heat to high and add the mushrooms and tomatoes. Stir-fry about 2 minutes. Add the seasoning sauce and stir another 1 minute or until the sauce has thickened.

7. Place the contents of the wok over the pasta. Mix briefly. Add the scallops; toss and serve immediately.

Any fresh pasta such as angel hair or capellini can be used.

If doubling this recipe, use two separate woks.

This pasta dish can be prepared ahead through step 2.

SERVES 2 to 4

Spinach Lo Mein

Sometimes students say to me, "I have all these drippings in the freezer and I forgot what you said to do with them." Make Spinach Lo Mein. Lo Mein means soft noodle. The Chinese don't make spinach noodles, so I am taking a little liberty when naming this dish.

¼ cup dried shiitake mushrooms
1 tablespoon reduced mushroom stock (see step 1)
1 cup mung bean sprouts

SEASONING SAUCE
2 teaspoons water chestnut powder
2 tablespoons medium-dry sherry
¼ cup defatted duck drippings
1 tablespoon oyster sauce
¼ cup Chicken Stock (see pp. 76–77)
1 tablespoon dark soy sauce

⅓ pound fresh spinach noodles
2½ tablespoons peanut oil
2 tablespoons minced shallots
1 teaspoon minced ginger
1 teaspoon minced garlic
½ cup shredded yellow Holland pepper
2 cups shredded bok choy, white and green parts included
1 cup snow peas, strung and left whole

1. Rinse the mushrooms under cold running water. In a small bowl, soak them in cold water to cover for about 1 hour or until soft. Squeeze them over the bowl. Set the mushrooms aside. Remove the stems and shred the mushrooms. Place the stems in a saucepan. Add the mushroom liquid. Reduce until 1 tablespoon remains. Strain the mushroom stock, then allow it to cool. Discard the stems.

2. Place the bean sprouts on paper towels to dry.

3. In a bowl, make the seasoning sauce by dissolving the water chestnut powder in the sherry, then adding the duck drippings, mushroom stock, oyster sauce, chicken stock, and soy sauce. Stir until well combined.

4. Bring a kettle of water to a rolling boil.

5. Preheat the oven to 250°.

6. Place a wok over high heat for about 1 minute or until it smokes. Add the bean sprouts. Allow them to scorch on one side for approximately 30 seconds, shaking the wok occasionally. Flip the bean sprouts in the wok and scorch them on the other side for another 30 seconds. Turn off the heat. Remove the bean sprouts to a plate.

7. Add the noodles to the boiling water and cook for 2 to 3 minutes. Drain the noodles in a colander. Shake the colander well to get rid of any excess water.

8. Return the wok to high heat. Add 1 tablespoon of the peanut oil. Add the drained noodles to the wok, and cook over high heat. Shake the wok occasionally but do not stir the noodles. Cook them about 1 to 2 minutes or until they scorch; then flip the noodles out of the wok onto a flat heatproof serving dish. Place them in the oven, uncovered.

9. Return the wok to low heat and add the remaining 1½ tablespoons peanut oil. Sauté the shallots for 2 minutes or until they soften. Add the ginger and the garlic; continue to sauté for 30 seconds. Turn the heat to high. Add the mushrooms, peppers, bok choy, and snow peas; stir-fry for 1 minute. Restir the seasoning sauce and add it to the wok all at once, continuing to stir-fry until the sauce thickens and has coated the vegetables. Turn off the heat. Add the bean sprouts. Stir briefly to mix. Remove the noodles from the oven and place the contents of the wok over the noodles. Serve immediately.

For the defatted duck drippings you can substitute Reduced Chicken Stock or Chicken Stock.

SERVES 2 to 3

Pasta with Fresh Wild Mushrooms

Don't let this recipe slip by. Pasta with Fresh Wild Mushrooms is speedy and simple, yet has a rich flavor from the shallots and wild mushrooms.

1 tablespoon unhulled sesame seeds
½ pound fresh wild mushrooms (preferably Italian cremini)
¾ cup small shallots

SEASONING SAUCE
1 tablespoon oyster sauce
1 tablespoon dark soy sauce
¼ cup Chicken Stock (see pp. 76–77)

BINDER
1 teaspoon water chestnut powder
2 tablespoons medium-dry sherry

1 tablespoon sweet butter
2 tablespoons peanut oil

⅓ pound fresh pasta
1 tablespoon Oriental sesame oil
½ cup snipped chives

1. Place a wok over high heat for about 1 minute or until it smokes. Add the sesame seeds. Turn the heat to low and dry-cook them for 3 to 5 minutes or until they brown. Empty the sesame seeds onto a flat plate.

2. Remove ½ inch from the stems of the mushrooms. Leave the mushrooms whole. Wash briefly under cold running water with a mushroom brush.

3. To make the shallots easier to peel, place them in a strainer and pour boiling water over them. Peel the shallots and leave whole.

4. Make the seasoning sauce by mixing together the oyster sauce, soy sauce, and chicken stock. Stir until well combined.

5. Make the binder by dissolving the water chestnut powder in the sherry. Stir until well combined.

6. Place a wok over high heat for a few seconds. Add the butter and turn the heat to low. Add the shallots and sauté over the lowest possible heat for about 10 to 20 minutes or until they are cooked through. The time will vary according to the size of the shallots.

7. Add the peanut oil to the wok and then the mushrooms. Sauté over low heat for about 7 minutes.

8. While the mushrooms are sautéing, cook the pasta in boiling water for approximately 2 to 3 minutes. The time will vary according to the thickness of the pasta you are using. When the pasta is done, drain in a colander.

9. Turn the heat to high, then add the seasoning sauce to the wok. Bring the sauce to a boil. Restir the binder and add it to the wok with one hand while stirring with the other. Cook a few seconds until the sauce thickens. Turn off the heat. Add the sesame oil and mix briefly.

10. Place the noodles on a flat heated serving dish. Pour the contents of the wok over the noodles. Sprinkle with sesame seeds and fresh chives. Serve immediately.

Any fresh pasta such as linguini or spaghetti can be used. Alternatively, dried pasta can be substituted.

This dish can be prepared early in the day through step 6.

SERVES 2 to 3

Linguini with Seafood Coriander Sauce

I love to serve this variation of Italian white clam sauce as a first-course pasta.

¼ pound small shrimp
¼ pound scallops
1 tablespoon olive oil
1½ tablespoons sweet butter
2 tablespoons minced shallots
1 teaspoon minced garlic
⅓ cup Chicken Stock, preferably salt-free (see pp. 76–77)
¼ cup finely chopped coriander leaves
3 teaspoons salt
    Freshly ground black pepper (10 turns of the mill)
2 tablespoons white wine
¼ pound dried linguini

1. Shell, split, devein, rinse, drain, and dry the shrimp on paper towels. Rinse and dry the scallops.

2. Place a wok over high heat for about 1 minute or until it smokes. Add the olive oil and, after a few seconds, the shrimp and scallops; stir-fry 1 minute. Remove the shrimp and scallops from the wok.

3. Turn the heat to low and add the butter. When the butter is melted, add the shallots and sauté for 2 minutes or until they have softened. Add the garlic and continue to sauté for another minute. Turn the heat to high. Add the chicken stock and bring to a simmer. Add the coriander, 1 teaspoon of the salt, the pepper, and the wine. Simmer another 2 minutes. Return the shrimp and scallops to the wok, along with any juices they have released. Turn off the heat.

4. Bring a medium-size kettle of water to a rolling boil. Add the remaining 2 teaspoons salt. Add the linguini and cook about 7 minutes or until tender but firm. Drain in a colander.

5. Bring the sauce to a simmer. Add the drained linguini. Toss well to coat. Turn off the heat. Serve immediately.

Use the freshest possible scallops, whether bay or sea. If the scallops you are using are large, quarter them.

Coriander is also known as cilantro or Chinese parsley.

This pasta dish can be prepared early in the day through step 2, in which case the shrimp and scallops should be refrigerated after they have been cooked.

When doubling or tripling this recipe, do not add more than ½ pound of scallops or shrimp to the wok at a time, lest they will stew instead of fry. Because the rate at which liquid evaporates is less rapid, do not double or triple the chicken stock, merely increase it by 2 tablespoons per recipe.

SERVES 2

Rice Noodles Primavera

In this recipe the popular Italian primavera sauce is en-livened by hot sauce and soy sauce, then paired with Chinese rice noodles.

¼ pound dried rice noodles
5 tablespoons olive oil
¼ cup minced shallots
½ cup slant-cut (⅛-inch thick) carrots
1 tablespoon minced garlic
1½ cups sliced fresh wild mushrooms
1½ cups slant-cut (1½-inch thick) bok choy, white and green
     parts included
¾ cup chopped well-ripened tomatoes
1½ cups snow peas, strung and left whole
¼ cup Chicken Stock, preferably salt-free (see pp. 76–77)
¾ cup Tomato Sauce (see pp. 16–17)
½ teaspoon Hot Sauce (see pp. 10–11)
1 tablespoon dark soy sauce
¼ cup chopped fresh basil
¼ cup heavy cream
1 teaspoon salt (optional)

1. Place the rice noodles in a bowl and cover with cold water for 30 minutes. Drain in a colander and toss with 1 tablespoon of the olive oil.

2. Preheat the oven to 250°.

3. Place a wok over high heat for about 1 minute or until it smokes. Add 2 tablespoons of the olive oil. Immediately add the rice noodles and stir-fry 2 minutes. Remove the noodles from the wok and place them on a heatproof serving dish. Place the serving dish in the oven without a cover.

4. Return the wok to low heat. Add the remaining 2 table-spoons olive oil and sauté the shallots for about 2 minutes or until

they soften. Add the carrots and garlic; continue to sauté for another minute. Add the mushrooms, bok choy, tomatoes, and snow peas. Turn the heat to high and stir-fry 1 minute. Pour the chicken stock around the sides of the wok and bring to a boil. Add the tomato sauce, Hot Sauce, and soy sauce; stir-fry until well combined. Turn the heat to low. Add the chopped basil and cream; stir 1 minute. Check for seasonings; add salt if desired.

5. Remove the noodles from the oven and pour the sauce over them. Serve immediately.

Rice noodles are made of rice and water. They are purchased dry in a package and can be stored in a glass jar or a plastic bag on the shelf for 1 year.

All the preparation for this dish can be done early in the day, but the cooking must be done at the last minute.

SERVES 2 to 4

Pasta with Eggplant and Oyster Mushrooms

I like this pasta creation so much that I do a variation on it, substituting grilled fresh shiitake mushrooms for the sautéed oyster mushrooms. If you choose to do this, here's how: Preheat the broiler or prepare a charcoal grill. Brush the shiitake mushrooms with melted butter and broil for about 5 minutes. Clip off the stems, then cut them in half or quarters depending on their size. Toss them in the wok along with the cooked pasta at the last moment.

1 small eggplant, weighing approximately 10 ounces
1 teaspoon salt
¼ pound fresh oyster mushrooms
2 tablespoons peanut oil
1 teaspoon minced ginger
2 tablespoons minced shallots
1 teaspoon minced garlic
2 tablespoons Reduced Chicken Stock (see pp. 76–77)
⅓ cup dry vermouth
½ teaspoon salt
Freshly ground black pepper (15 turns of the mill)
¼ cup heavy cream

2 teaspoons salt
⅓ pound fresh thin pasta

1. Cut the unpeeled eggplant diagonally into thin slices. Place the slices on top of each other, cut them into strips, and then dice them small. The yield should be 2 cups diced eggplant. Spread the diced eggplant on a flat plate. Sprinkle with 1 teaspoon salt. Cover the eggplant with a paper towel, then place a heavy skillet on top. Allow the weighted eggplant to sit for 1 hour or until

a few tablespoons of water have been extracted. Place the eggplant pieces in a colander, then rinse, drain, and dry them very well.

2. Rinse the oyster mushrooms briefly under cold running water. Cut off and discard the hard part of the stems. Cut the mushrooms into strips.

3. Bring a large kettle of water to a rolling boil.

4. While the water is coming to a boil, place a wok over high heat for about 1 minute or until it smokes. Add the peanut oil; heat for a few seconds. Add the eggplant and stir-fry a few seconds then press the eggplant down with the back of a spatula for 3 minutes. Allow the eggplant to scorch slightly.

5. Add the mushrooms, ginger, and shallots; stir-fry 1 minute. Add the garlic, continuing to stir a few seconds. Add the Reduced Chicken Stock and vermouth. Bring to a boil and reduce by half. Add the ½ teaspoon salt and pepper. Stir briefly, then add the cream. Turn the heat to low and simmer another minute. Turn off the heat.

6. Add the 2 teaspoons salt to the kettle of boiling water, then add the pasta. Cook for about 2 to 3 minutes. Drain in a colander.

7. Bring the sauce in the wok to a simmer. Add the drained pasta and toss until it is well coated with the sauce. Serve immediately.

This pasta dish can be prepared early in the day through step 2.

SERVES 2

Chinese Roasted Pepper Pasta

This simple light pasta creation, which is a by-product of Hunan Roasted Peppers, makes a great side dish or first-course pasta served hot or at room temperature.

2 tablespoons peanut oil
1 tablespoon minced garlic
⅓ cup sliced (⅛-inch rounds) scallions, white and green parts included
2 tablespoons chopped coriander leaves
1 cup Hunan Roasted Peppers with their juice (see page 129)
1 tablespoon Chicken Stock (see pp. 76–77)
½ teaspoon Hot Sauce (see pp. 10–11)
1 tablespoon Oriental sesame oil

2 teaspoons salt
⅓ pound fresh lo mein

1. In a 10-inch skillet, heat the peanut oil until it is hot but not smoking. Turn the heat to low and sauté the garlic and scallions until the garlic just begins to brown.

2. Add the coriander and stir briefly. Add the Hunan Roasted Peppers and their juice, continuing to stir. Add the chicken stock and cook for another minute. Add the Hot Sauce and sesame oil. Stir briefly, then turn off the heat.

3. Bring a large kettle of water to a rolling boil. Add the salt, then the fresh lo mein. Cook 2 to 3 minutes. Drain in a colander.

4. Bring the sauce to a simmer. Add the drained pasta to the simmering sauce. With the heat on high, stir and toss 1 minute or until the sauce is well combined with the pasta. Turn off the heat. Serve hot or at room temperature.

Any fresh pasta such as linguini or spaghetti can be substituted for the lo mein.

This pasta dish can be prepared several hours in advance.

SERVES 2

Linguini with Chinese Ratatouille

This is a simple pasta dish you can throw together in a few minutes, but only when you are trying to use up the last cup of Chinese Ratatouille.

1 cup Chinese Ratatouille (see pp. 130–131)
1 cup Tomato Sauce (see pp. 16–17)
2 teaspoons salt
⅓ pound dried linguini
½ cup freshly grated Parmesan cheese

1. Chop the Chinese Ratatouille into smaller pieces.
2. Place a 10-inch skillet over medium heat and add the tomato sauce and ratatouille, stirring until well combined. Turn off the heat.
3. Bring a kettle of salted water to a rolling boil. Add the linguini and cook about 7 minutes or until tender but firm. Drain in a colander.
4. Bring the sauce to a simmer. Add the drained linguini to the sauce. Stir well to coat. Turn off the heat. Add the Parmesan cheese; toss well. Serve immediately.

This recipe can be prepared ahead through step 2.

SERVES 2

Grilled Vegetable Pasta

This recipe came about when I had some leftover grilled vegetables that I wanted to use up. Pasta is the perfect foil for leftovers.

1 eggplant, weighing about 1 pound
3 or 4 small zucchini, weighing about 1 pound
1 red sweet pepper
1 yellow Holland pepper
¼ pound fresh shiitake mushrooms

MARINADE
3 tablespoons light soy sauce
3 tablespoons dark soy sauce
1 tablespoon unhulled sesame seeds
3 tablespoons Oriental sesame oil
2 teaspoons sugar

1 pound dried whole wheat Udon noodles
1 pound smoked mozzarella cheese, diced
⅓ cup sliced (⅛-inch rounds) scallions, white and green
    parts included

1. Cut off and discard the ends of the eggplant, then cut the eggplant into ½-inch-thick circles. Cut the zucchini in the same manner, then triangle-cut the peppers. Remove the stems from the mushrooms (reserve for when you are making stock).
2. Make the marinade by combining the light and dark soy sauces, sesame seeds, sesame oil, and sugar in a bowl. Place the eggplant, zucchini, peppers, and mushrooms in a shallow roasting pan. Using a pastry brush, coat each side with the marinade. Allow to marinate 1 hour.
3. Preheat the broiler for 15 minutes.
4. Bring a large kettle of water to a rolling boil.
5. Broil the vegetables in the roasting pan for 5 minutes on

one side. Turn the pan around and the vegetables over. Broil another 5 minutes on the other side or until they are cooked through and charred on the outside. Remove the vegetables from the broiler. Quarter the eggplant and mushrooms.

6. Add the Udon noodles to the kettle of boiling water and cook 5 to 6 minutes or until tender but firm. Drain the noodles then place them in a pasta bowl. Working quickly, add the mozzarella cheese and the scallions to the pasta. Toss well until the cheese has almost melted. Stir in the vegetables along with 4 tablespoons of marinade from the roasting pan. Serve immediately.

If you can't find smoked mozzarella, you can substitute the fresh.

Udon are Japanese whole wheat noodles. You can substitute any dried pasta such as linguini.

This pasta dish can be prepared early in the day through step 5.

SERVES 6 to 8

Sichuan Peppercorn Linguini

This speedy little side dish of spicy pasta is great to serve with a subtle fish entrée, such as Sautéed Sole with Ginger Sauce or Parchment Salmon in Ginger Saffron Sauce.

1 cup mung bean sprouts
⅓ pound dried linguini
1 tablespoon Oriental sesame oil

SEASONING SAUCE
1 tablespoon dark soy sauce
1 tablespoon hoisin sauce
1 teaspoon Hot Sauce (see pp. 10–11)
2 teaspoons honey
1 teaspoon Sichuan Peppercorn Powder (see page 13)

1 tablespoon peanut oil
⅓ cup sliced (⅛-inch rounds) scallions, white and green
     parts included
¼ cup diced sweet red pepper
¼ cup diced yellow Holland pepper
2 teaspoons minced garlic
2 teaspoons minced ginger

1. Place the bean sprouts on paper towels to dry.

2. Bring a kettle of water to a rolling boil. Add the linguini and cook until tender but firm. Drain the linguini in a colander, then rinse under cold running water. Toss with sesame oil.

3. Place a wok over high heat for about 1 minute or until it smokes. Add the bean sprouts. Allow them to scorch on one side for approximately 30 seconds, shaking the wok occasionally. Flip the bean sprouts in the wok and scorch them on the other side for another 30 seconds. Turn off the heat. Remove the bean sprouts to a plate.

4. Make the seasoning sauce by combining the soy sauce, hoisin sauce, Hot Sauce, honey, and Sichuan Peppercorn Powder in a bowl.

5. Return the wok to high heat. Add the peanut oil and heat for a few seconds. Add the scallions, red and yellow peppers, garlic, and ginger. Stir over high heat for about 1 minute. Add the seasoning sauce, stirring well. Turn off the heat.

6. Add the drained linguini to the wok. Mix with the sauce and toss until the pasta and the sauce have been well combined. Add the charred bean sprouts and toss again briefly. Serve hot or at room temperature.

This pasta dish can be prepared in its entirety several hours in advance.

SERVES 2

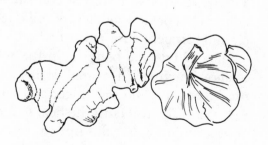

Scallion Ginger Crepes

Serve these crepes as an accompaniment to Barbecued Roast Chicken or Sichuan Peppercorn Roast Duck. Roll or fold the crepes alongside the bird.

CREPE BATTER
1 cup cold water
1 cup cold milk
4 eggs
½ teaspoon salt
2 cups sifted flour
4 tablespoons sweet butter, melted

1 tablespoon sweet butter
3 tablespoons minced ginger
½ cup sliced (⅛-inch rounds) scallions, white and green
   parts included

2 tablespoons peanut oil

1. Place the water, milk, eggs, and salt in the bowl of a food processor. Using the on-and-off technique, process until the mixture is well combined. Add the flour and turn the processor on and off a few more times. Add the melted butter, continuing to turn the processor on and off until the batter is smooth. Use an icing spatula around the sides of the bowl to incorporate any bits of flour that have not been combined. Process a few more seconds. The batter should have the consistency of light cream, just thick enough to coat a wooden spoon. Pour the batter into a lidded glass jar and refrigerate for at least 2 hours.

2. While the batter is in the refrigerator, make the ginger-scallion mixture: In a small skillet, heat the 1 tablespoon butter until it foams. Add the ginger and sauté 2 minutes over low heat. Add the scallions. Turn the heat to medium and continue to sauté another minute. Set this mixture aside until cooled.

3. When you are ready to cook the crepes, pour the batter into a bowl, then stir in the ginger-scallion mixture.

4. Preheat the oven to 350°.

5. *To Make the Crepes:* Place a 6- to 6½-inch cast-iron skillet, crepe, or omelet pan over moderately high heat for about 1 minute. Add ½ tablespoon of the oil. Circulate it around the skillet, then pour out the excess, so that only a thin film is coating the pan. Pour a scant ¼ cup of the batter into the pan. Reduce the heat to low. Rotate the skillet so that a thin circular pancake is formed. After a few seconds, lift the edges with a metal icing spatula; if the crepe is light brown, flip it. Remove the crepe to a heatproof plate. Repeat the cooking procedure until all the crepes have been made. Pile the cooked crepes on top of each other like a stack of pancakes. Keep warm in the oven for 5 to 7 minutes, uncovered. Fold into quarters before serving.

Scallion Ginger Crepes can be made up to 1 day in advance and reheated in a 350° oven on a heatproof dish for about 5 minutes. I like them even better reheated, because the perimeter of the crepes becomes crunchy.

YIELDS: 20 crepes

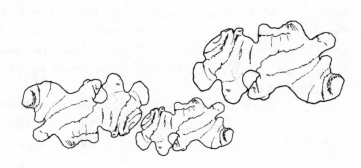

Chinese Hero

This invention was inspired by an article Mimi Sheraton wrote for Time *Magazine on the American fascination with sandwiches. A Chinese hero can, of course, be made for lunch, but I find it also is a conversation piece when served as an appetizer for an informal gathering of friends.*

1 cup mung bean sprouts
1 crusty loaf Italian bread
2 tablespoons mayonnaise
2 Chinese Napa cabbage leaves
1 well-ripened plum tomato, sliced
1 whole scallion, shredded
¼ pound Barbecued Roast Loin of Pork, sliced (see pp. 268–269)
⅓ cup Hunan Roasted Peppers (see page 129)
1 tablespoon Spicy Mustard Sauce (see page 14)

1. Place the bean sprouts on paper towels to dry.

2. Cut off a section of one end of the bread so that the loaf is 9 inches long. Split the loaf in half lengthwise, then remove the center of the bread (save the center for another use, for instance bread crumbs).

2. Cut off a section of one end of the bread so that the loaf is 9 inches long. Split the loaf in half lengthwise, then remove the center of the bread (save the center for another use, for instance bread crumbs).

3. Place a wok over high heat for about 1 minute or until it smokes. Add the bean sprouts. Allow them to scorch on one side for about 30 seconds, shaking the wok occasionally. Flip the bean sprouts in the wok and scorch them on the other side for another 30 seconds. Turn off the heat. Remove the bean sprouts to a plate and allow to cool.

4. Using one piece of the bread as the bottom layer of the hero, spread the mayonnaise over it. Add the Chinese-Napa cabbage leaves. On top of this, layer the tomato slices in an overlap-

ping pattern. Sprinkle the shredded scallion over the tomato slices. Cover this completely with an overlapping layer of Barbecued Roast Loin of Pork. Add the Hunan Roasted Peppers. Finally, top with the slightly charred bean sprouts. Spread the Spicy Mustard Sauce on the other piece of the bread, then place this half on the sandwich. Slice the hero into quarters and serve.

If you live near a Chinese community, you can purchase barbecued roast pork already made. Alternatively you can substitute Westphalian, Black Forest, or smoked country ham.

SERVES 2–6

Candied Walnut and Scallion Bread

The Chinese don't have ovens in the home, so the bread they usually make is steamed. Since Americans favor the old crusty loaf, I wanted to bake a bread but add a Chinese touch. One day I came across a recipe for Walnut and Onion Bread in James Beard's book Beard on Bread. *I substituted scallions and candied walnuts with excellent results.*

5 to 6 cups all-purpose unbleached flour
1 tablespoon salt
2 tablespoons sugar
2 cups milk
1 package active dry yeast
½ cup walnut oil
¾ cup Candied Walnuts, roughly chopped (see page 126)
¾ cup sliced (⅛-inch rounds) scallions, white and green
   parts included

Butter for greasing

1. Sift 5 cups of the flour into a large bowl. Add the salt and sugar.
2. Place the milk in a saucepan and heat over low heat until it is warm (105° to 115°). Remove the saucepan from the heat.
3. Place the yeast in a cup and pour in ½ cup of the warm milk. Stir until the yeast is dissolved. Pour this mixture into the middle of the flour. Stir in the walnut oil and mix briefly with chopsticks. Add the rest of the milk, continuing to stir. Knead well on a flat surface for about 10 minutes or until the dough is firm and blended into a smooth, springy ball. Add up to 1 cup more flour if the dough is sticky. Place the dough in a clean bowl, cover with a dry tea towel, and allow to rise in a warm place for 2 hours or until it has doubled in bulk. To test for double in bulk, press

the tips of two fingers lightly and quickly ½ inch into the dough. If the dents stay, it is double.

4. Punch down the dough in the bowl by pushing your fist into the center, then pulling the edges of the dough to the center. Turn the dough over and remove it from the bowl. Place it on a flat surface. Add the walnuts and scallions, kneading them into the dough until they are well distributed. Cut the dough into 4 equal parts with a cleaver and shape them into 4 rounds. Place the 4 loaves on a greased flat cookie sheet. Cover the loaves with a dry tea towel. Allow to rise for 45 minutes.

5. Preheat the oven to 375°.

6. Bake the loaves for 10 minutes at 375°, then turn the oven down to 350° and continue to bake another 20 to 30 minutes or until the loaves are well browned and sound hollow when tapped underneath.

7. Allow the loaves to cool on a rack for at least 20 minutes before slicing. Waiting to eat the bread is the hardest part of the recipe.

I let my bread rise in the linen closet, which provides a warm environment.

YIELDS 4 small loaves

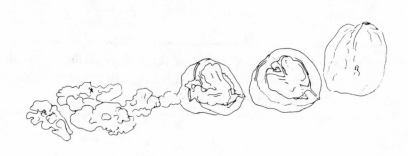

Candied Walnuts

In addition to using these Candied Walnuts for the Candied Walnut and Scallion Bread, I serve them with cocktails, for dessert with fresh fruit, or crushed on top of ice cream. They are also wonderful just to eat on their own.

½ pound shelled walnuts
6 tablespoons sugar

2 cups peanut oil for deep-frying

1. In a saucepan, bring 1 quart of water to a rapid boil over high heat. Add the walnuts. Boil them over medium heat for 5 minutes. Turn off the heat. Drain the nuts in a strainer placed over the sink, then return them to the saucepan on the burner. If using an electric range, place the saucepan on a cool burner.
2. Leave the heat off. Working quickly, add the sugar and mix well. Place a lid on the saucepan and allow the sugar to melt for 1 minute.
3. Place the walnuts on a plate in a single layer and allow them to dry for 10 minutes.
4. Place a 12-inch wok over high heat for about 1 minute or until it smokes. Pour in the oil; turn the heat to medium and bring the oil to 350°. Using a wire strainer, lower the walnuts into the oil and deep-fry them for about 2 minutes or until the sugar coating has caramelized. In order to achieve an even brown color, stir the walnuts constantly while they are frying. Remove the walnuts with a wire strainer and place them in a single layer on a brown paper bag to drain. Allow them to cool before serving.

Candied Walnuts can be made several days in advance. In the unlikely event that there are any left over, they can be stored in a glass jar in the refrigerator for one month.

SERVES 8 to 10

Vegetables

HUNAN ROASTED PEPPERS

CHINESE RATATOUILLE

DEEP-FRIED BOK CHOY LEAVES

SNOW PEAS WITH CORIANDER AND
BLACK SESAME SEEDS

PICKLED GINGER

PINE NUT RICE STUFFED TOMATOES

MINIATURE VEGETABLES WITH SHALLOTS
AND CREMINI MUSHROOMS

BROCCOLI DE RAPE WITH OYSTER MUSHROOMS

BRUSSELS SPROUTS WITH HAM
AND CANDIED GINGER

STIR-FRIED WATERCRESS WITH
WOK-SEARED TOMATOES

Hunan Roasted Peppers

The Chinese answer to Italian roasted peppers is this versatile dish that can be added to pasta sauces, sandwiches, rice dishes, stir-fried shrimp, and more. By themselves, these make a great room-temperature hors d'oeuvre.

1½ pounds triangle-cut sweet peppers (combination of red, green, and yellow), 4 full cups cut
1 teaspoon salt

SEASONING SAUCE
1 tablespoon light soy sauce
1 teaspoon Hot Sauce (see pp. 10–11)
2 teaspoons red wine vinegar
½ teaspoon sugar

1½ tablespoons peanut oil

1. Place the peppers on a cookie sheet and sprinkle them with salt. Cover with paper towels, then put a weight over the towels. Let them stand at least 2 hours. Drain and dry the peppers.

2. Make the seasoning sauce by mixing together the soy sauce, Hot Sauce, vinegar, and sugar. Stir until well combined.

3. Place a wok over high heat for about 1 minute or until it smokes. Add the peanut-oil; heat until hot but not smoking.

4. Add the peppers; stir-fry 4 to 5 minutes, pressing down on them with a spatula to aid the scorching. If they are scorching too fast, reduce the heat. The scorched skin of the peppers gives them the charcoal flavor, so the peppers should be charred.

5. Add seasoning sauce; stir-fry until all the liquid is absorbed. Empty into serving dish. Serve at room temperature.

Be sure to dry the peppers well. Otherwise they will not scorch in the wok. The scorching determines the success of the dish.

Refrigerate Hunan Roasted Peppers for up to 1 week.

SERVES 6

Chinese Ratatouille

Sometimes I place alternating eggplant, peppers, and mushrooms on a bamboo skewer or in a leaf of Belgian endive and serve Chinese Ratatouille as an hors d'oeuvre. Other times I serve it as part of a room-temperature buffet, or as a vegetable accompaniment to hamburgers, roast chicken, or leg of lamb. It can also be made into a pasta dish, Linguini with Chinese Ratatouille. Once I added the last ¾ cup to Chinese Vegetable Risotto instead of the Hunan Roasted Peppers that are called for. This dish gets around.

¼ cup dried Chinese mushrooms
1 tablespoon reduced mushroom stock (see step 1)
1 medium-size eggplant (1 pound)
2 teaspoons salt

SEASONING SAUCE
1 teaspoon Hot Sauce (see pp. 10–11)
1 tablespoon dark soy sauce
1 tablespoon red wine vinegar
1 teaspoon sugar
⅓ cup Tomato Sauce (see pp. 16–17)
2 tablespoons medium-dry sherry

3 tablespoons peanut oil
2 teaspoons minced garlic
2 whole scallions, cut into ⅛-inch rounds
½ cup triangle-cut red sweet pepper
½ cup triangle-cut yellow Holland pepper
¼ cup Chicken Stock (see pp. 76–77)

1. Rinse the mushrooms under cold running water. In a small bowl, soak them in cold water to cover for about 1 hour or until soft. Squeeze them over the bowl. Remove the stems and

quarter the mushrooms. Set the mushrooms aside. Place the stems in a saucepan. Add the mushroom liquid. Reduce until about 1 tablespoon remains. Strain the mushroom stock and reserve; discard the stems.

2. Trim the ends of the eggplant and discard. Quarter the eggplant lengthwise, then cut each quarter into 4 long strips. Slice each strip into 1-inch cubes. Sprinkle the eggplant cubes with the salt. Place them on a cookie sheet, cover with a paper towel and place a chopping block on top. Let stand for 30 minutes or longer. Then rinse, drain, and dry the eggplant cubes well.

3. Make the seasoning sauce by mixing together the Hot Sauce, soy sauce, vinegar, sugar, tomato sauce, and sherry. Stir until well combined.

4. Place a wok over high heat for about 1 minute or until it smokes. Add the peanut oil and heat until hot but not smoking. Add the eggplant cubes; stir and press lightly to aid browning. Cook over medium-high heat for about 3 minutes or until the eggplant cubes have begun to soften and show signs of charring.

5. Add the garlic, scallions, red and yellow peppers, and the reserved mushrooms; stir-fry for 2 minutes. Restir the seasoning sauce and add it to the wok, continuing to stir another minute. Add the mushroom stock and the chicken stock around the sides of the wok. Continue to stir-fry until all of the juices have been absorbed into the eggplant mixture. Empty the contents of the wok onto a serving dish. Allow to cool at least 6 hours before serving. Serve at room temperature.

Please make this dish early in the day or up to 5 days in advance. The texture and flavor really improves with age. Allow it to reach room temperature before serving.

SERVES 5 to 6

Deep-fried Bok Choy Leaves

This simple, decorative condiment is so good it often up-stages the dish it surrounds. It is very versatile and can be used as a garnish for appetizers such as Shrimp and Icicle Radish Toast, Wild Mushroom Spring Rolls, or Shanghai Vegetarian Spring Rolls. You can also serve it with meat, fish, or poultry dishes that have no colorful vegetables.

10 to 15 large intensely green bok choy leaves
 2 cups peanut oil
 1 teaspoon salt
 1 teaspoon sugar
 1 teaspoon dried bonito flakes

1. Do not wash the bok choy leaves unless they are sandy. If you must wash them, make sure they are bone dry before frying. Pile the bok choy leaves on top of each other and shred finely.

2. Place a wok over high heat for about 1 minute or until it smokes. Add the peanut oil and heat until the oil reaches 375°. If you don't have a deep-fat frying thermometer, you can stand a chopstick upright in the middle of the wok; the oil is ready when bubbles form rapidly around the chopstick. Place a handful of bok choy leaves in the wok. Deep-fry for 1 to 2 minutes or until they are crisp but before they start to turn brown. Using a wire strainer, remove the bok choy leaves from the oil and drain on several layers of very absorbent paper towels. Reheat the oil to 375° and repeat the procedure, deep-frying one handful of bok choy leaves at a time until all the leaves have been fried.

3. Sprinkle the drained bok choy with salt, sugar, and bonito flakes. Serve the bok choy leaves immediately or within a few hours, in which case serve them at room temperature.

Bonito flakes are a Japanese dried fish. They are sold in Oriental markets as well as many supermarkets.

SERVES 2 to 4

Snow Peas with Coriander and Black Sesame Seeds

A stir-fried vegetable makes a great low-calorie as well as nutritious lunch. This particular dish also has black sesame seeds, which are an excellent source of calcium.

2 teaspoons black sesame seeds
1 tablespoon Oriental sesame oil
¼ cup sliced (⅛-inch rounds) scallions, white and green parts included
1 teaspoon minced ginger
1 teaspoon minced garlic
3 cups snow peas, strung and left whole
1 tablespoon light soy sauce
1 tablespoon dark soy sauce
2 tablespoons chopped coriander leaves

1. Place a wok over high heat for about 1 minute. Add the sesame seeds. Turn the heat to low and dry-cook them for 3 to 5 minutes or until they release a nutty scent. Empty the sesame seeds onto a flat plate.

2. Place a wok over high heat for about 1 minute or until it smokes. Add the sesame oil and then, immediately after, add the scallions, ginger, and garlic. Stir-fry about 30 seconds.

3. Add the snow peas and stir-fry 1 minute. Add the light and dark soy sauce and mix a few seconds. Add the coriander and mix a final few seconds. Empty the contents of the wok onto a serving plate, and sprinkle with black sesame seeds. Serve hot, warm, or at room temperature.

SERVES 3 to 4

Pickled Ginger

There are two different types of ginger, spring (also called young or baby) and winter. Ginger grows in the ground. If the ginger is picked when the leaves are still green, it is called spring ginger. After the leaves turn brown, it becomes winter ginger.

Spring ginger has a thinner skin, with a pink cast, and is much milder in flavor than the winter variety. It is usually available in August and September, only to be found in Chinese communities. I have seen it in the springtime, but not with any regularity. The only way you can prepare spring ginger for long-term storage is to pickle it. Once pickled, it will last 2 years in the refrigerator.

Besides the convenience of storing it, I love to pickle ginger because, with its more subtle flavor, it is more versatile in cooking. Fresh ginger would not work well in a salad dressing but pickled ginger works beautifully, as in Pickled Ginger Vinaigrette.

1 pound winter or spring ginger

PICKLING SOLUTION
½ cup sugar
1 cup Japanese rice vinegar
1 cup water

1. Peel the ginger, then slice it paper thin.
2. Bring a large pot of water to a rolling boil.
3. Make the pickling solution by mixing together the sugar, vinegar, and water. Stir until the sugar is dissolved.
4. Place the ginger slices in the boiling water for 1 minute, then remove them with a wire strainer.
5. While the ginger is still hot, place it in the pickling solution. Allow to cool, then place the ginger slices with the pickling solution in several glass jars with tight-fitting covers. Refrigerate.

You don't have to pickle winter ginger. It can be stored by first peeling it and then placing it in sherry. Use this sherry when a recipe calls for sherry and then when the level goes down, replenish with new sherry. It should always be covered. Stored in the refrigerator, it will last 1 year.

A jar of pickled ginger makes a great gift for a knowledgeable cook. This is the ginger that the Japanese use when serving sushi.

The ginger will take on a pink cast when it is placed in the pickling solution while still hot.

Ginger Tea has become one of my favorite drinks. Place about 1½ cups of water in a small saucepan. Add 2 or 3 slices (¼ inch thick) of unpeeled fresh ginger in the saucepan and boil uncovered for 5 minutes. Pour the ginger tea into a cup through a tea strainer. Add a dash of lemon juice and a teaspoon of honey. I used to drink ginger tea only when I had a cold or sore throat, but now I drink it all the time. It has no calories (except for the honey, which can be left out) and none of the caffeine you get with coffee or tea.

When choosing winter ginger, pick out a nice fat piece, with smooth skin and no wrinkles.

If you don't want to make your own, you can substitute a good-quality commercial pickled ginger, such as Sushi Chef.

YIELDS 1 quart

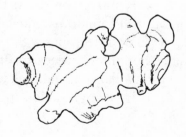

Pine Nut Rice Stuffed Tomatoes

This simple rendition of stuffed tomatoes can be assembled early in the day and then baked just before serving. They are a great accompaniment to many entrées, including broiled fish or roasted meat or poultry.

¼ cup pine nuts
6 medium-size ripe tomatoes
1 teaspoon salt
1 tablespoon sweet butter
2 whole scallions, cut into ⅛-inch rounds
1 teaspoon minced garlic
1 cup chopped bok choy, white and green parts included
1½ cups cooked and cooled Kokuho Rose rice
2 tablespoons olive oil
2 teaspoons dark soy sauce
1 teaspoon Hot Sauce (see pp. 10–11)
  Butter for greasing
1 cup grated sharp cheese, such as Asiago or any good
  sharp cheddar

Special Equipment
Cheesecloth

1. Preheat the oven to 325°. Place the pine nuts on a cookie sheet and roast for 5 to 10 minutes or until they are golden brown. Set aside.
2. Turn the oven to 350°.
3. Remove the stem, then cut off a ½-inch slice from the top of each tomato. Remove the seeds and most of the pulp, leaving a ½-inch-deep base. Sprinkle the inside of the tomatoes with salt. Allow more juices to drain by turning the tomatoes upside down on a flat roasting rack while preparing the stuffing.
4. In a small skillet, melt 1 tablespoon butter until it foams.

Add the scallions and garlic; sauté 2 minutes. Turn off the heat and set aside.

5. Place the chopped bok choy in a piece of cheesecloth that has been wrung out in cold water. Squeeze hard to extract the excess moisture.

6. Place the bok choy, scallions, garlic, cooked rice, pine nuts, olive oil, soy sauce, and Hot Sauce in a bowl. Mix well with chopsticks. Stuff the tomatoes and place them in a greased shallow roasting pan, allowing a little space between each.

7. Bake the tomatoes uncovered for about 10 to 12 minutes or until they are cooked through but before the skin starts to pull away from the tomatoes. Remove them from the oven.

8. Turn the oven to broil. Distribute the grated cheese equally over the tops of the tomatoes. Place the tomatoes, still in the same shallow roasting pan, under the broiler and broil another 2 minutes or until the cheese has melted. Serve immediately.

For the Kokuho Rose rice, which is a short-grained Japanese rice, any cooked rice can be substituted.

SERVES 6

Miniature Vegetables with Shallots and Cremini Mushrooms

I got the idea of sautéing whole shallots from the French. Shallots are the royalty of the onion family and, when sautéed whole, are given the billing they deserve. Cremini are Italian mushrooms that are grown in the Po Valley of northern Italy. When shallots and cremini are combined with a stir-fry of miniature vegetables, the result is fit for a Chinese banquet.

1 cup whole small shallots
1 tablespoon sweet butter
¾ pound miniature vegetables (summer squash variety)
2 cups small whole fresh cremini mushrooms

SEASONING SAUCE
1 teaspoon water chestnut powder
2 tablespoons medium-dry sherry
¾ tablespoon dark soy sauce
¾ tablespoon oyster sauce

2 tablespoons olive oil
⅓ cup Chicken Stock, preferably salt-free (see pp. 76–77)

1. Place the shallots in a strainer and pour boiling water over them to loosen the skins. Peel the shallots and leave whole. Place a wok over high heat for about 1 minute. Turn the heat to low. Add the butter and, immediately after, the shallots. Sauté the shallots over the lowest possible heat for about 20 minutes or until they are brown and have cooked through. The time may vary according to the size of the shallot. Turn off the heat. This step may be done several hours in advance.

2. Steam the miniature vegetables for 2 minutes or until they have softened but still have some crunch. Remove them from the

steamer. To stop the cooking and hold the color, plunge them into a bowl of ice-cold water for about a minute or until they cool. Drain them in a colander set over a bowl. After they are dry, remove the stem ends.

3. Remove about ½ inch of the stems of the cremini mushrooms. Rinse the mushrooms under cold running water briefly while lightly brushing with a mushroom brush. Drain the mushrooms, but leave whole. If small mushrooms are not available, then quarter larger ones lengthwise.

4. Make the seasoning sauce by dissolving the water chestnut powder in the sherry, soy sauce, and oyster sauce. Stir until well combined.

5. Turn the heat to high under the wok that contains the shallots. Add the oil. Immediately after, add the miniature vegetables; stir-fry 2 minutes. Add the cremini and continue to stir-fry another 2 minutes. Add the stock around the sides of the wok. Bring it to a boil and allow it to reduce a few seconds. Restir the seasoning sauce and add it to the wok all at once, continuing to stir-fry about 2 minutes or until the sauce forms a glaze. Empty the contents of the wok onto a serving dish and serve immediately.

For the cremini, you can substitute fresh shiitake mushrooms, chanterelles, or American cultivated mushrooms.

When miniature vegetables are not available, you can substitute roll-oblique cut zucchini and yellow squash.

This dish can be prepared early in the day through step 4.

SERVES 4

Broccoli de Rape with Oyster Mushrooms

Broccoli de rape is Italian broccoli that is similar to Chinese broccoli, as they both have a slightly bitter taste. It is in season in the fall and early winter. If you wish to prepare this dish at another time of the year, you can substitute either Chinese or American broccoli.

The other featured ingredient, oyster mushrooms, are so called because they have both the taste and the shape of an oyster. They grow wild in temperate regions and are now being widely cultivated in the Orient, Europe, and America.

¾ pound bunch broccoli de rape
⅓ pound fresh oyster mushrooms

SEASONING SAUCE
1 teaspoon water chestnut powder
2 tablespoons medium-dry sherry
1 tablespoon oyster sauce
1 tablespoon dark soy sauce
¼ teaspoon Hot Sauce (see pp. 10–11)

2 tablespoons peanut oil
1 whole scallion, cut into 1-inch rounds
1 teaspoon minced garlic

1. While the bunch of broccoli de rape is still tied, cut off and discard 2 inches of the stems. Holding the entire bunch together, cut the broccoli into 2½-inch pieces. Wash and drain. Steam the broccoli for two minutes or until it has softened but still has some crunch. Remove it from the steamer. To stop the cooking and hold the color, plunge it into a bowl of ice-cold water for about a minute or until it cools. Drain the broccoli in a colander set over a bowl.

2. Clean the oyster mushrooms with a pastry or mushroom brush. Cut off and discard the hard part of the stems. Cut the remaining part of the stems crosswise thinly. Cut the mushrooms into thick strips, maintaining their shape. If small, leave whole.

3. Make the seasoning sauce by first dissolving the water chestnut powder in the sherry, then adding the oyster sauce, soy sauce, and Hot Sauce. Stir until well combined.

4. Place a wok over high heat for about 1 minute or until it smokes. Add the peanut oil and heat for a few seconds. Add the mushroom stems; stir-fry 1 minute. Add the mushrooms and scallions; stir-fry 1 minute. Add the garlic, stir-frying another few seconds. Add the broccoli de rape; continue to stir-fry another minute or until the broccoli is covered with oil.

5. Restir the seasoning sauce and add it to the wok all at once, continuing to stir-fry another few seconds or until the sauce has glazed the broccoli. Empty the contents of the wok into a serving dish and serve immediately or at room temperature.

Broccoli de Rape with Oyster Mushrooms can be prepared early in the day through step 3.

SERVES 3 to 4

Brussels Sprouts with
Ham and Candied Ginger

This is a most delicious and interesting way to use up leftover ham. You can also buy a piece of Virginia ham or other country smoked ham.

3½ cups brussels sprouts

SEASONING SAUCE
  3 tablespoons medium-dry sherry
 ⅓ cup Chicken Stock, preferably salt-free (see pp. 76–77)
1½ tablespoons Dijon mustard
1½ tablespoons finely chopped candied ginger
  1 tablespoon ham drippings (optional)

BINDER
  1 teaspoon water chestnut powder
 ½ tablespoon medium-dry sherry

  2 tablespoons peanut oil

  2 whole scallions, cut into ⅛-inch rounds
 ¼ pound country smoked ham, trimmed and triangle-cut

  1 teaspoon Oriental sesame oil

1. Cut off and discard ¼ inch of the stem of each brussels sprout. Make a crisscross cut into each stem. Steam the brussels sprouts for about 5 minutes or until they have softened but still have some crunch. Remove them from the steamer. To stop the cooking and hold the color, plunge them into a bowl of ice-cold water for about a minute or until they cool. Drain them in a colander set over a bowl.

2. Make the seasoning sauce by mixing together the 3 table-spoons sherry, chicken stock, mustard, candied ginger, and ham drippings. Continue to stir until the mixture has been well combined.

3. Make the binder by dissolving the water chestnut powder in the ½ tablespoon sherry. Stir until well combined.

4. Place a wok over high heat for about 1 minute or until it smokes. Add the peanut oil and heat for a few seconds. Add the scallions; stir-fry a few more seconds. Add the brussels sprouts and stir-fry for 2 minutes. Add the ham and mix briefly. Restir the seasoning sauce and add it to the wok all at once; bring to a boil. Restir the binder and add it to the wok, continuing to stir. Cook the sauce until it thickens, another minute or two. Turn off the heat and stir in the sesame oil. Empty the contents of the wok into a serving dish. Serve immediately.

If you have baked a ham, save those brown crusty drippings and juices (not the fat) to add to this dish.

This dish can be prepared early in the day through step 3.

SERVES 2 to 3

Stir-fried Watercress with Wok-Seared Tomatoes

This recipe was inspired by Jeremiah Towers' restaurant, Star's, in San Francisco. He serves it with a smoked loin of pork. I like to serve it with my Barbecued Roast Loin of Pork. However, Stir-fried Watercress with Wok-Seared Tomatoes is a vegetable dish that's fit for any occasion.

1 tablespoon unhulled sesame seeds
4 bunches watercress
2 tablespoons peanut oil
1 teaspoon minced garlic
2 whole scallions, cut into ⅛-inch rounds
1 teaspoon minced ginger
1 teaspoon salt
Freshly ground black pepper (10 turns of the mill)
2 cups well-ripened cherry tomatoes, halved

1. Place a wok over high heat for about 1 minute or until it smokes. Add the sesame seeds. Turn the heat to low and dry-cook them for 3 to 5 minutes or until they brown. Turn off the heat. Empty the sesame seeds onto a flat plate.

2. While the watercress is still tied, cut off and discard 2 inches of the stems. Wash the watercress then spin-dry.

3. Place the wok over high heat for about 1 minute or until it smokes. Add the peanut oil and heat for a few seconds. Add the garlic, scallions, ginger, salt, and pepper; stir-fry 1 minute. Add the watercress and stir-fry 1 more minute or until it wilts. Empty the contents of the wok.

4. Return the wok to high heat. Add the tomatoes and stir-fry another minute. You will hear a searing noise as the tomatoes begin to char. Return the watercress to the wok and mix well for a few seconds to combine all the ingredients. Empty the contents of

the wok onto a serving platter and sprinkle with sesame seeds. Serve immediately.

All the preparation for this dish can be done early in the day, but the cooking must be done at the last minute.

SERVES 3 to 4

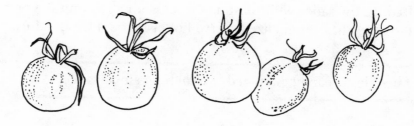

Five Spice Braised Leeks

8 medium-size leeks

SEASONING SAUCE
½ teaspoon five spice powder
¼ cup medium-dry sherry
2 tablespoons dark soy sauce
2 teaspoons honey
1½ cups Chicken Stock, preferably salt-free (see pp. 76–77)
4 tablespoons sweet butter

1. Trim the root ends of the leeks close but not so close that the layers separate. Cut away a portion of the green part of the leeks so that each leek will be about 7 or 8 inches long. Reserve the greens for stock or Tomato Sauce. Lay the leeks flat on a cutting surface and split them in half lengthwise almost all the way through (up to within an inch of the root), making sure they do not separate. Using a vegetable brush, rinse the leeks under warm running water to remove all sand. Drain.

2. Make the seasoning sauce by mixing together the five spice powder, sherry, soy sauce, and honey.

3. Place the leeks, chicken stock, and butter in an oven-proof skillet with a cover and simmer over low heat with the cover askew for 30 minutes. The liquid should be almost evaporated.

4. Preheat the oven to 350°.

5. Add the seasoning sauce to the leeks, then place them in the oven. Cook the leeks without a cover for another 20 minutes.

6. Remove the skillet from the oven. Place over high heat. Reduce the sauce while basting the leeks for a few minutes or until the sauce has caramelized. Serve hot or at room temperature.

These leeks can be prepared several hours in advance.

SERVES 4

Five Spice Baked Acorn Squash

For me acorn squash is as important a part of the fall as tomatoes are an important part of the summer. When choosing them, look for deep green color with one irregular orange spot. At its best, acorn squash has an interior that is a deep pumpkin color with an intensely sweet and rich taste. I like to eat Five Spice Baked Acorn Squash alone for lunch occasionally or with dinner, served with Peking Turkey or Barbecued Roast Loin of Pork.

1 medium-size acorn squash
¼ teaspoon five spice powder
1 tablespoon sweet butter
1 tablespoon minced Ginger in Syrup (see page 294)

1. Before preheating the oven, place the top rack in the center of the oven and the bottom rack in the lower third of the oven. Place a shallow roasting pan containing 1 inch of water on the lower rack. Preheat the oven to 350°. Prick the acorn squash with a poultry skewer, then place it on the top rack. Bake for 1 hour or until the squash is cooked through. Test by piercing it with the poultry skewer. Remove the squash from the oven.

2. Split the squash in half and scoop out the seeds. Place half the butter in the center of each. Sprinkle with five spice powder. Place the squash on a heat-proof enamel platter, then place under the broiler, about 3 inches from the heat source. Broil at 350° for 10 to 15 minutes.

3. Sprinkle on the ginger and serve immediately.

If desired, you can bake the squash several hours in advance. The broiling should be done just before serving.

SERVES 2

Napa Cabbage with Seared Onions and Sun-Dried Tomatoes

This dish is at once beautiful, healthy, tasty, and simple.

1 whole Chinese Napa cabbage, weighing 2 pounds
1 Spanish onion, weighing approximately 1 pound

BINDER
1 teaspoon water chestnut powder
1 tablespoon medium-dry sherry

1 tablespoon sweet butter
1 teaspoon salt
1½ tablespoons olive oil
2 cloves garlic, crushed

¼ cup diced sun-dried tomatoes
1 tablespoon oil from sun-dried tomatoes

1. Remove a few of the outside leaves of the cabbage. Cut the cabbage in half lengthwise, then rinse under cold running water and drain. Cut each cabbage half 2 or 3 times lengthwise and then, from one end to the other, make a crosswise cut every 1½ inches.

2. Cut the onion in half lengthwise; peel, then slice thin.

3. Make the binder by dissolving the water chestnut powder in the sherry. Stir until well combined.

4. Place a cast-iron skillet over high heat for about 1 minute. Add the butter. Turn the heat to medium. When the butter has melted, add the onions and ½ teaspoon of the salt; sauté for about 10 minutes or until the onions have scorched. Turn off the heat.

5. Place a wok over high heat for about 1 minute or until it smokes. Add the olive oil, the remaining ½ teaspoon salt, and then

the garlic. Turn the heat to low and let the garlic sizzle a few seconds. Add the cabbage and stir-fry over high heat for about 2 to 3 minutes or until the cabbage begins to soften.

6. Restir the binder and add it to the wok with one hand while stir-frying with the other. Continue to stir-fry until the juices have thickened, about 30 seconds. Place the cabbage in the center of a flat serving dish. Place the seared onions around the cabbage to form a border. Sprinkle the sun-dried tomatoes on top of the cabbage, then drizzle the oil from the sun-dried tomatoes over the cabbage and serve immediately.

This dish can be prepared early in the day through step 3.

SERVES 4

Seafood

SAUTÉED SOLE WITH GINGER SAUCE

GRILLED TUNA WITH FRESH
TOMATO LIME SAUCE

FRESH TOMATO LIME SAUCE

BROILED SWORDFISH WITH SHALLOTS
AND LONG BEANS

STUFFED RED SNAPPER IN PARCHMENT

PARCHMENT SALMON IN
GINGER SAFFRON SAUCE

GINGER SESAME GRILLED SALMON

STEAMED NORWEGIAN SALMON WITH
BLACK BEAN SAUCE

WOK-CHARRED NORWEGIAN SALMON

SHRIMP WITH FAVA BEANS

CHINESE SCAMPI

BROILED SHRIMP WITH ASPARAGUS
AND ALMONDS

CHARRED SHRIMP WITH HUNAN PEPPERS

SCALLOPS IN GINGER SAUCE

STIR-FRIED SHRIMP NOODLES
WITH LUMP CRABMEAT

SHRIMP NOODLES

EASTERN JAMBALAYA

STEAMED LOBSTER WITH
BLACK BEAN GINGER MAYONNAISE

SOFT-SHELL CRABS IN GARLIC SAUCE

SOFT-SHELL CRABS WITH SCALLIONS
AND PICKLED GINGER

LOBSTER WITH SCALLIONS AND
PICKLED GINGER

GINGER BUTTER GRILLED LOBSTER

TEA SMOKED LOBSTER WITH
LEMON CAPER SAUCE

CHINESE LOBSTER FRA DIAVOLO

LOBSTER CANTONESE WITH CAVIAR

SHAD ROE AND ASPARAGUS WITH
GINGER BUTTER SAUCE

Sautéed Sole with Ginger Sauce

A true spur-of-the-moment dish, Sautéed Sole with Ginger Sauce is speedy, delicious, low in calories, and nutritious.

1 pound fresh sole fillet (2 pieces)
¼ cup flour for dredging
2 tablespoons medium-dry sherry
1 tablespoon dark soy sauce
3 tablespoons peanut oil
1 tablespoon sweet butter
1 tablespoon very finely shredded ginger
3 tablespoons minced shallots
¼ cup Chicken Stock, preferably salt-free (see pp. 76–77)

GARNISH
Lemon twists (see illustration, page 158)

1. Preheat the oven to 250°. Place a serving dish in the oven.
2. Rinse, drain, and dry the fillet of sole. Dip the fillets in flour and shake off the excess.
3. In a small bowl, combine the sherry and the soy sauce.
4. Place a skillet over high heat for about 1 minute. Add the oil and heat until hot but not smoking. Place the fillets in the skillet in a single layer. Sauté about 2 minutes, shaking the skillet occasionally to avoid sticking. Turn the fillets over and sauté another 2 minutes. Turn off the heat. Transfer the fillets to the heated serving dish, then place them in the oven to keep warm, uncovered.
5. Pour off any excess oil from the skillet. Turn the heat to low. Add the butter and heat until melted. Sauté the ginger and shallots for 1 minute over low heat.
6. Pour in the stock and turn the heat to high. Bring the stock to a boil and simmer for 1 minute.
7. Add the sherry and soy sauce mixture all at once, stirring until the sauce thickens slightly. Pour the sauce over the fish fillets. Garnish with lemon twists. Serve immediately.

SERVES 2

Grilled Tuna with Fresh Tomato Lime Sauce

Remember when fish was cooked "until it flakes"? No more! This grilled tuna should be served medium-rare. If it is served well done, it will be hard and dry, more so with fresh tuna than almost any other fish I have found. Buy a thick piece so that a crust develops.

MARINADE
1 tablespoon dark soy sauce
1 tablespoon olive oil
½ teaspoon grated lime zest
1 tablespoon fresh lime juice
½ teaspoon minced garlic
1 teaspoon Spicy Mustard Sauce (see page 14)
1 whole scallion, cut into ⅛-inch rounds
1 teaspoon minced ginger

One 1-pound piece tuna fillet, triangle-shaped, cut about 1½-inches thick
1 recipe Fresh Tomato Lime Sauce (see page 156)

1. Make the marinade by combining the soy sauce, olive oil, lime zest, lime juice, garlic, Spicy Mustard Sauce, scallion, and ginger in a bowl.

2. Place the tuna fillet in the bowl and massage it with the marinade on both sides. Allow the tuna to marinate for 4 to 6 hours in the refrigerator.

3. While the tuna is marinating, make the Fresh Tomato Lime Sauce.

4. Prepare the charcoal grill or preheat the broiler. If you are cooking outdoors, grill the tuna 3 minutes on one side, then turn the tuna and grill another 3 minutes on the other side. If you

are using an oven broiler system, broil the tuna on one side for 6 minutes, as close to the heat source as possible.

5. Serve the tuna alone or with accompanying Fresh Tomato Lime Sauce.

The marinade works beautifully on swordfish, yellowtail, tilefish, salmon, or almost any thick fish fillet.

An alternate method of preparing this dish is to cut the fish into large cubes and skewer it.

If you are broiling the tuna inside, choose a heat-proof dish in which you can marinate, broil, and serve the fish. I use the covers from oval-shaped enamel Dutch ovens.

Leftover pieces of this grilled tuna can be turned into a fresh tuna salad by adding mayonnaise, lime juice, capers, dill, and fresh chives.

SERVES 2

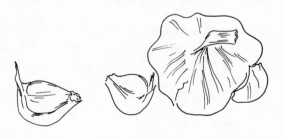

Fresh Tomato Lime Sauce

    7 plum tomatoes
    1 tablespoon olive oil
    1 tablespoon sweet butter
    1 tablespoon lime juice
    ¼ teaspoon salt
       Freshly ground black pepper (10 turns of the mill)
    ¼ cup snipped chives

1. To loosen the tomato skin, plunge the tomatoes, 1 or 2 at a time, into rapidly boiling water to cover. Blanch them for 10 seconds, then drain immediately. Remove the stem, then, starting at the stem end, peel off the skin from each tomato. Cut the tomatoes in half widthwise. Remove the seeds and lightly squeeze out the juice. Dice.

2. Place a skillet over high heat. Add the olive oil and butter; heat until the butter foams. Sauté the tomatoes over high heat for 3 to 4 minutes. Pour in the lime juice and continue to sauté another minute over medium heat. Add the salt and pepper.

3. Place the tomato sauce in a bowl and sprinkle with chives. Serve with the Grilled Tuna.

This sauce is also excellent without cooking the tomatoes, in which case you would not need the butter.

Fresh Tomato Lime Sauce can be prepared early in the day.

YIELDS approximately 2 cups

Broiled Swordfish with Shallots and Long Beans

If you are on your way home from work and you feel like having a piece of broiled fish for dinner with a little pizzazz, this recipe will definitely fill the bill. Accompanied by a steaming bowl of rice, you will have a delicious dinner that requires only minutes.

One 1-pound swordfish steak, 1 inch thick

MARINADE
- 1 tablespoon dark soy sauce
- 3 tablespoons medium-dry sherry
- 1 tablespoon Oriental sesame oil
- 1 tablespoon unhulled sesame seeds
- 2 teaspoons minced ginger
- 2 whole scallions, cut into ⅛-inch rounds
- 1 teaspoon minced garlic

- 10 small shallots
- 1 tablespoon sweet butter
- ¼ pound Chinese long beans

1. Preheat the oven to broil for 20 minutes.
2. Rinse the swordfish steak under cold running water. Drain and pat dry with paper towels. Place the swordfish on a heatproof dish.
3. Make the marinade by mixing together the soy sauce, sherry, sesame oil, sesame seeds, ginger, scallions, and garlic. Stir until well combined, then pour the marinade over the swordfish. Allow to marinate while you are preparing the rest of the dish.
4. To make the shallots easier to peel, place them in a strainer and pour boiling water over them. Peel the shallots and leave whole. Heat the butter in a skillet until it melts. Add the

shallots and sauté over the lowest possible heat for 15 to 20 minutes or until they are brown and have cooked through.

5. While the shallots are sautéing, steam the long beans 3 to 4 minutes or until they have softened but still have some crunch. Remove them from the steamer. To stop the cooking and hold the color, plunge the long beans into a bowl of ice cold water for about a minute or until they cool. Drain them in a colander set over a bowl. After the beans are dry, remove the stem ends.

6. Broil the swordfish 1 inch from the heat source for 8 to 10 minutes. Do not turn. Remove the swordfish from the broiler and place it on an oval-shaped serving platter. Arrange the long beans around the swordfish, then place the shallots on top of the long beans. Pour the natural sauce left in the dish in which the fish was broiled over the swordfish. Serve immediately.

You can choose almost any type of thick fish fillet as a substitute, including salmon, tuna, red snapper, or tilefish.

You can prepare this several hours in advance through step 5.

SERVES 2

Stuffed Red Snapper in Parchment

I love to bake fish in parchment paper. As you don't need special equipment, it is less complicated than steaming, and as the juices are condensed and contained in the wrapping, there is no need to reduce or thicken the sauce.

1 whole red snapper, weighing 2 to 2½ pounds

STUFFING
2 medium-size dried Chinese mushrooms
½ pound shrimp
1 small leek
1 teaspoon minced ginger
¼ pound ground pork
1½ tablespoons light soy sauce

BINDER FOR STUFFING
1 teaspoon water chestnut powder
1 tablespoon medium-dry sherry
1 tablespoon peanut oil

SEASONING SAUCE
1 tablespoon dark miso
1 tablespoon hoisin sauce
1 tablespoon dark soy sauce
1 tablespoon Oriental sesame oil
2 tablespoons medium-dry sherry
1 teaspoon Hot Sauce (see pp. 10–11)
1 teaspoon brown sugar

3 thin slices ginger
2 whole scallions, cut into 1-inch pieces

SPECIAL EQUIPMENT
Cooking parchment paper
Unwaxed dental floss

1. Have the fishmonger remove the backbone of the red snapper but leave the fish whole with the head and tail intact (the fish will look as if it were butterflied). Rinse the fish under cold running water and dry on paper towels.

2. *To Prepare the Stuffing:* Rinse the mushrooms, cover with cold water, and soak for 1 hour or until soft. Squeeze the excess liquid from the mushrooms. Cut the mushrooms in half; remove and discard the stems. Then cut them into small dice.

3. Shell, devein, rinse, drain, dry, and dice the shrimp.

4. Remove the root end of the leek, then split the leek in half lengthwise all the way through. Place it under forcefully running warm water to remove all traces of sand. Then cut the white and also the tender light green part into ½-inch pieces (reserve the dark green part for Tomato Sauce or stock). The yield should be ½ cup chopped leeks.

5. Place the mushrooms, leeks, and ginger in a bowl on a tray. Place the pork, light soy sauce, and shrimp in individual bowls on the tray.

6. Make a binder by dissolving the water chestnut powder in 1 tablespoon sherry. Mix until well combined.

7. *To Cook the Stuffing:* Place a wok over high heat for about 1 minute or until it smokes. Add the peanut oil and heat for a few seconds. Add the pork and stir-fry for 2 to 3 minutes or until it turns white. Add the mushrooms, leeks and ginger; stir-fry 1 more minute. Add the light soy sauce and mix briefly. Restir the binder and add it to the wok with one hand while stirring with the other for another 30 seconds. Turn off the heat and empty the contents of the wok onto a plate. Add the shrimp to the stuffing and mix well.

8. Make the seasoning sauce by placing the miso, hoisin sauce, dark soy sauce, sesame oil, 2 tablespoons sherry, Hot Sauce, and brown sugar in a bowl. Mix until well combined.

9. Preheat the oven to 375°.

10. Center the fish skin-side down and opened up on a piece of cooking parchment paper that is 6 inches longer than the fish. The paper should extend 3 inches beyond the head and 3 inches beyond the tail. Place the stuffing on top of the fish from head to tail. Close the fish up tightly. Do not overstuff. If some of the

stuffing falls out, this is fine. With unwaxed dental floss, tie the fish at the head and at least 3 other places along the body. Place the sliced ginger and scallions on top of the fish. Lift the parchment paper containing the fish and place it in an oven-proof dish with a lip. Pour the seasoning sauce over the fish. Envelop the fish in the parchment first lengthwise: Fold the paper over the fish then seal by rolling and pinching the edges tightly together. Secondly, close up each end by making 2 triangular folds (as if gift wrapping), then seal the edge by rolling and pinching.

11. Place the wrapped fish in a shallow roasting pan and bake for 20 minutes.

12. Remove the fish from the oven. Clip the dental floss and remove. Serve the fish in the parchment.

For the red snapper you can substitute sea bass.

This dish can be prepared early in the day through step 8.

SERVES 2

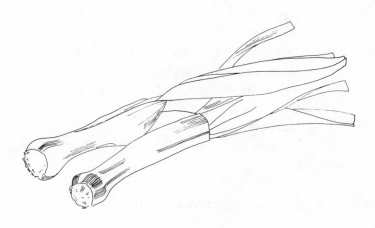

Parchment Salmon in Ginger Saffron Sauce

Every once in a long while a recipe this good and this simple comes along. The preparation takes about 5 minutes, and the taste is as subtle as it is extraordinary, a perfect blending of Eastern and Western seasonings.

For the salmon fillet you can substitute tilefish fillet. This recipe also works beautifully with a whole red snapper or a sea bass, in which case you would make three crescent-shaped incisions on both sides of the fish. I sometimes prepare this dish using a whole side of a salmon fillet, which usually weighs 2½ to 3 pounds.

There are two important things you must remember when making these substitutions: adjust both the timing and the seasonings. The timing varies according to the thickness of the fish. A whole red snapper or sea bass weighing 2 to 2½ pounds or a whole side of a salmon require 16 to 20 minutes. If your fish weighs more, increase the seasonings accordingly.

  2 tablespoons sweet butter
 ⅛ teaspoon crushed saffron
 ½ teaspoon curry powder
One 1-pound piece salmon fillet, about 1 inch at its thickest point
  1 tablespoon lime juice
  2 teaspoons minced ginger
  1 whole scallion, cut into ⅛-inch rounds
  1 tablespoon Pernod
 ½ teaspoon salt
    Freshly ground black pepper (8 turns of the mill)

SPECIAL EQUIPMENT
Cooking parchment paper

1. Preheat the oven to 375°.

2. In a saucepan, melt the butter over low heat until it foams. Turn off the heat. Add the saffron and the curry powder. Allow this mixture to steep uncovered for 15 minutes or longer.

3. Pull out any remaining bones from the salmon with your fingers, using a paper towel to grip.

4. Place the salmon on cooking parchment paper, leaving 6 inches of extra paper at both ends. Pour the seasoned butter over the salmon. Add the lime juice, then the ginger. Sprinkle the scallions on top. Dribble the Pernod over the fish. Add salt and pepper. Wrap the fish by bringing 2 edges of the parchment over the fish. Pinch the paper together at the top, then pinch and fold all the way down toward the fish. Roll the 2 remaining ends of parchment down and under so that the fish is tightly sealed.

5. Place the salmon in a heat-proof shallow dish and bake it in the oven for 12 to 15 minutes. Garnish with scallion brushes as illustrated below. Serve immediately.

Parchment Salmon in Ginger Saffron Sauce can be prepared early in the day through step 3, and through step 4 one hour in advance.

SERVES 2

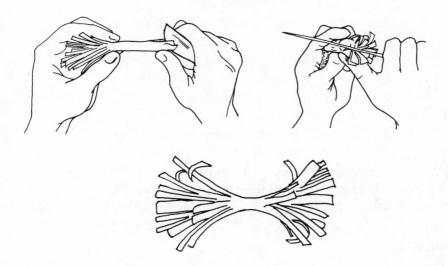

Ginger Sesame Grilled Salmon

*This dish makes you look like an expert but you only have
to be a beginner. Garnished with lemon twists and scallion
brushes, Ginger Sesame Grilled Salmon has graced many
a buffet table for my catering assignments, looking like a
masterpiece when it is actually the simplest recipe in this
entire book.*

1 whole side Norwegian salmon fillet,
　　weighing about 3 pounds

MARINADE
3 tablespoons unhulled sesame seeds
½ cup medium-dry sherry
3 tablespoons dark soy sauce
3 tablespoons Oriental sesame oil
2 tablespoons minced ginger
¾ cup whole scallions, cut into ⅛-inch rounds
1 tablespoon minced garlic

GARNISH
Scallion brushes (see illustration, page 163)
Lemon twists (see illustration, page 169)

　　1. Rinse the salmon under cold running water then pat dry
with paper towels. Using a paper towel to grip, remove any remaining bones. Place the salmon fillet skin-side down in an oblong,
shallow 12 by 17 metal roasting pan.
　　2. Make the marinade by mixing together the sesame seeds,
sherry, soy sauce, sesame oil, ginger, scallions, and garlic. Stir
until well combined. Spoon the marinade over the salmon and
allow it to marinate at room temperature for 1 hour.
　　3. Adjust the broiler tray in the oven so that it is 4 inches
from the heat source. Preheat the oven to broil for at least 10
minutes.

4. Broil the salmon for 10 minutes or until it has almost cooked through but before it shows signs of cracking (broil less if you want it medium-rare). If the salmon is unusually thick (over 1½ inches), broil for 10 minutes, then reduce the oven temperature to 450° and bake the salmon on the middle shelf of the oven for an additional 5 minutes. In either case, do not turn the salmon over. While the salmon is cooking, check at least 2 times to see that the juices are not burning. If the juices are evaporating too fast, splash in a little sherry.

5. Remove the salmon fillet from the roasting pan with two fish spatulas that are at least 4 inches wide. Place on a white, flat, oval serving platter. Garnish with alternating scallion brushes and lemon twists. Pour the few tablespoons of fish juices accumulated in the roasting pan over the salmon fillet. If there are more than a few tablespoons, reduce the juices in the roasting pan over direct heat until only a few tablespoons remain. Serve hot or at room temperature.

A whole side of salmon fillet is long and wide, so you will definitely need 2 wide fish spatulas to remove it from the roasting pan.

For the salmon you can substitute many different kinds of fish as long as they are thick fillets, such as: swordfish, tuna, tilefish, fluke, or red snapper. If the choice is salmon, this dish works beautifully served at room temperature.

You can also choose a 1-pound salmon steak; marinate, broil, and serve it in the same dish. If you use a smaller piece of fish, adjust the marinade and timing accordingly.

SERVES 6 to 8

Steamed Norwegian Salmon with Black Bean Sauce

Frequently a student signing up for a course will ask, "Are we going to learn how to make Cantonese black bean sauce?" It is a long-time favorite with Americans, for even those who swear they will only eat Sichuan-style cooking. Paired with a rich-tasting fish such as salmon, black bean sauce makes this dish really outstanding.

One 1¼-pound piece of Norwegian salmon fillet, skin removed on both sides
  1 tablespoon medium-dry sherry

1½ tablespoons fermented black beans, minced
  1 teaspoon minced ginger
  1 teaspoon minced garlic
  2 whole scallions, cut into ⅛-inch rounds

BINDER
  1 teaspoon water chestnut powder
  2 tablespoons medium-dry sherry
  2 teaspoons dark soy sauce

  1 tablespoon peanut oil
⅓ cup Chicken Stock, preferably salt-free (see pp. 76–77)
  1 teaspoon Oriental sesame oil

1. Rinse then dry the salmon fillet on paper towels. Place the salmon in an oval-shaped dish with a lip (to catch the juices). Spoon 1 tablespoon sherry over the salmon.

2. In a bowl combine the black beans, ginger, garlic, and scallions.

3. Make the binder by first dissolving the water chestnut powder in the 2 tablespoons sherry, then adding the soy sauce. Stir until well combined.

4. Set up a steamer by placing a high-legged rack in the bottom of a dome-shaped enamel turkey roaster. Fill the roaster with about 2½ inches of water. Place the dish containing the salmon on top of the rack. Cover the roaster, turn the heat to high, and allow the water to come to a boil. After the water is boiling, steam the salmon for 8 to 10 minutes. Remove the salmon from the steamer and pour the salmon juices into a Pyrex cup and reserve.

5. Place a wok over high heat for about 1 minute or until it smokes. Add the peanut oil and heat for a few seconds. Add the black bean mixture and stir-fry for about 1 minute. Add the reserved salmon juices and chicken stock; bring to a boil. Simmer 1 minute.

6. Restir the binder, then add it to the wok with one hand while stirring with the other. Turn off the heat. Add the sesame oil. Stir briefly. Pour the sauce over the salmon and serve immediately.

My favorite way to serve this dish is in small portions as an appetizer, in which case it serves 4 to 6.

Steaming is a delicate, low-calorie, healthy way to prepare fish.

Norwegian Salmon is a first choice, but you can substitute any fresh salmon that is available.

SERVES 2 to 6

Wok-Charred Norwegian Salmon

This Nouvelle Chinese version of Louisiana Blackened Red Fish uses fresh herbs as opposed to dried and a wok for the blackening method instead of a cast-iron skillet. It must be a well-seasoned wok and heated for the full 5 minutes called for in the recipe.

One 1-pound piece Norwegian salmon fillet, no more than 1 inch at the thickest point, skin removed on both sides
2 tablespoons sweet butter, melted

MARINADE
2 teaspoons minced garlic
2 teaspoons minced coriander leaves
2 teaspoons minced ginger
½ teaspoon salt
Freshly ground black pepper (30 turns of the mill)

GARNISH
Lemon twists (see opposite page)

1. Rinse then dry the salmon fillet on paper towels. Place it on a plate.
2. In a small saucepan melt the butter over low heat. Allow it to cool.
3. Make the marinade by mixing together the garlic, coriander, ginger, salt, and pepper. Stir until well combined.
4. Pour equal amounts of the melted butter over each side of the salmon fillet. Rub equal amounts of the marinade on each side. Allow to marinate at room temperature for 30 minutes.
5. Place a wok over high heat for 5 minutes. Open all the windows, as this dish will create a lot of smoke. Place the salmon in the center of the wok and cook over high heat for 3 minutes. After about 30 seconds, loosen the salmon with a spatula, then shake the wok to ensure that the salmon does not stick. Shake it

again after about another minute. If any of the marinade has stuck to the plate, smooth it over the salmon. Using a fish spatula, turn the salmon over and cook an additional 3 minutes, shaking the wok occasionally. Turn off the heat. Remove the salmon to a serving dish. Garnish with lemon twists and serve immediately.

For the salmon, you can substitute fresh tuna or swordfish.

SERVES 2

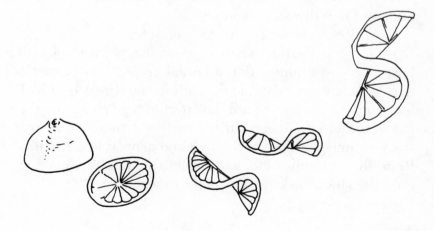

Shrimp with Fava Beans

Pairing pink shrimp with a green vegetable is always a good idea. My first choice for this dish is fava beans, also called broad beans because of their broad, plump shape. If fava beans are not in season, you can substitute broccoli, asparagus, brussels sprouts, or snow peas. If using snow peas, steam only 1 minute.

1 pound medium shrimp (21–25 to the pound)

SEASONING SAUCE
1 teaspoon water chestnut powder
2 teaspoons medium-dry sherry
1 tablespoon dark soy sauce

1¼ pounds fresh fava beans, shelled
2 tablespoons peanut oil
3 tablespoons minced shallots
2 tablespoons minced Pickled Ginger (see pp. 134–135)
¼ cup Chicken Stock, preferably salt-free (see pp. 76–77)

1. Shell, split, devein, rinse, drain, and dry the shrimp on paper towels.
2. Make the seasoning sauce by dissolving the water chestnut powder in the sherry and soy sauce.
3. Steam the fava beans for 5 minutes.
4. While the fava beans are steaming, place a wok over high heat for about 1 minute or until it smokes. Add the peanut oil and heat for a few seconds. Add the shrimp and stir-fry over high heat for about 2 minutes or until they start to turn pink. Add the shallots and Pickled Ginger; stir-fry another 2 minutes. Pour in the stock around the sides of the wok and allow it to come to a boil. Restir the seasoning sauce and add it to the wok all at once, stirring until the sauce thickens. Turn off the heat.

5. Place the fava beans in the center of a round white serving dish. Arrange the ginger shrimp around the beans. Serve immediately.

SERVES 2 to 3

Chinese Scampi

This Chinese version of Italian Scampi served in steamed bok choy leaves is light, tasty, and colorful.

1½ pounds medium-large shrimp (20 to the pound)

MARINADE
1 tablespoon medium-dry sherry
1 teaspoon light soy sauce

3 to 4 large bok choy leaves
2 tablespoons peanut oil
1 teaspoon minced garlic
⅓ cup sliced (⅛-inch rounds) scallions, white and green
    parts included
1 teaspoon minced ginger
¼ cup medium-dry sherry
1 tablespoon dark soy sauce
    Freshly ground black pepper (20 turns of the mill)
1 tablespoon chopped coriander leaves
1 teaspoon Oriental sesame oil

1. *To Butterfly the Shrimp* (see illustration opposite): Remove the shells, except for the last segment of the tail. Cut the shrimp along the convex side, but do not let the knife go all the way through the meat. Devein the shrimp. With the tip of a boning knife, make a widthwise slit about 1 inch long in the middle of each shrimp on the convex side. Push the tail of the shrimp into the slit, then pull the tail through to the other side. The purpose of butterflying is to prevent the shrimp from curling up when cooked. Rinse the shrimp under cold running water, then drain and pat dry.

2. Make the marinade by mixing together the sherry and light soy sauce.

3. Mix the shrimp with the marinade, then place it in the refrigerator for at least 1 hour or up to 12 hours.

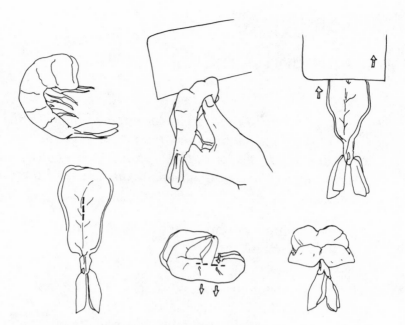

4. Preheat the broiler for 20 minutes.

5. Steam the bok choy leaves for 1 minute, then place them on a flat serving dish.

6. Place the shrimp on a heat-proof platter, tails up, and broil as close as possible to the heat source for 2 to 3 minutes or until the tails are slightly charred and the shrimp turn pink.

7. While the shrimp are broiling, place a wok over high heat for about 1 minute or until it smokes. Add the peanut oil and heat for a few seconds. Add the garlic, scallions, and ginger; stir-fry 1 minute. Add the ¼ cup sherry, dark soy sauce, and pepper; stir a few seconds. Remove the shrimp from the broiler and add them to the wok, along with the coriander. Stir-fry a few seconds over the highest possible heat. Place the contents of the wok on the bok choy leaves. Dribble sesame oil over the shrimp and serve immediately.

This dish can be prepared early in the day through step 3.

SERVES 3

Broiled Shrimp with Asparagus and Almonds

By broiling the shrimp, I have eliminated the necessity of marinating and passing them through oil, making the dish speedier and less caloric. This dish is a great choice for the springtime when asparagus are at the height of their season.

 1 pound medium shrimp (21–25 to the pound)
1½ pounds asparagus
 SEASONING SAUCE
1½ teaspoons water chestnut powder
 2 tablespoons medium-dry sherry
 ¼ cup Chicken Stock, preferably salt-free (see pp. 76–77)
 1 tablespoon dark soy sauce
 1 teaspoon Hot Sauce (see pp. 10–11)

 ¼ cup almonds
 2 tablespoons peanut oil
 2 teaspoons minced garlic
 3 whole scallions, cut into ⅛-inch rounds
 2 teaspoons minced ginger

1. Preheat the oven to 325°.
2. *To butterfly the shrimp,* see page 173.
3. To determine the tender portion of the asparagus, hold the bottom of each individual stalk in the left hand, in a gently closed fist. With the right hand, palm open, slap the green stalks so that they break cleanly. Roll-oblique cut the tender portion of the asparagus. The yield should be approximately 4 cups.
4. Make the seasoning sauce by first dissolving the water chestnut powder in the sherry, then adding the chicken stock, soy sauce, and Hot Sauce. Stir until well combined.

5. Place the almonds on a cookie sheet and roast in the preheated oven for 10 minutes or until they are golden brown. Remove them from the oven and set aside.

6. Turn the oven to broil. Place the shrimp on an oval-shaped heatproof dish and run under the broiler for about 4 minutes or until they have turned pink. This procedure can also be done on an outdoor barbecue.

7. While the shrimp are broiling, place a wok over high heat for about 1 minute or until it smokes. Add the peanut oil and heat for a few seconds. Add the asparagus and stir-fry over medium heat for 4 to 5 minutes. Turn the heat to high. Add the garlic, scallions, and ginger; stir-fry 1 minute.

8. Restir the seasoning sauce and add it to the wok all at once, continuing to stir until the sauce thickens. Remove the shrimp from the broiler and pour the asparagus mixture into the center of the shrimp so that the shrimp form a border. Garnish with roasted almonds. Serve immediately in the same dish in which the shrimp were broiled.

This dish can be prepared early in the day through step 5.

SERVES 2 to 3

Charred Shrimp with Hunan Peppers

Cooking shrimp in the shell has long been a Chinese technique for acquiring optimum flavor.

    1 pound medium shrimp (21 to 25 to the pound)
    2 tablespoons peanut oil
  ½ cup shredded scallions, white and green parts included
    1 tablespoon minced garlic
1½ cups Hunan Roasted Peppers, measured with their juice
        (see page 129)

1. Using a pair of scissors, cut (but do not remove) the shell along the back of the shrimp. Cut off the legs. Devein, then rinse the shrimp under cold running water. Drain, then place the shrimp on a cookie sheet lined with paper towels; allow to dry for 1 hour, changing the paper towels several times. If they are not perfectly dry, they will not char.

2. Place a wok over high heat for about 1 minute or until it smokes. Add ½ tablespoon of the peanut oil and heat for another few seconds. Add half the shrimp. Shaking the wok occasionally, allow the shrimp to char for about 1½ minutes. Turn the shrimp over and char another 1½ minutes. Remove the shrimp from the wok. Add another ½ tablespoon of peanut oil to the wok and repeat the procedure with the remaining shrimp. Remove the shrimp from the wok.

3. Add the remaining 1 tablespoon of oil to the wok. Stir-fry the scallions and garlic over high heat for about 30 seconds.

4. Return the charred shrimp to the wok and stir-fry another 30 seconds.

5. Add the Hunan Roasted Peppers and stir-fry 30 seconds or until the peppers and shrimp are well combined. Serve hot or at room temperature.

Keep a batch of Hunan Roasted Peppers on hand in order to complete this tasty dish.

Serve these charred shrimp as a first course.

SERVES 3 to 4

Scallops in Ginger Sauce

Scallops in Ginger Sauce is traditionally served hot. To avoid the last-minute attention required, an alternative would be to serve it as a room-temperature salad in individual lettuce leaf portions. Handled this way, you can make the entire dish several hours in advance and serve it as a first course for dinner or as a main-course salad for lunch.

1 pound scallops

MARINADE
1 tablespoon water chestnut powder
1 tablespoon medium-dry sherry
1 egg white

SEASONING SAUCE
1 teaspoon water chestnut powder
2 tablespoons medium-dry sherry
1 tablespoon dark soy sauce
½ tablespoon light soy sauce
1 teaspoon balsamic vinegar
1 teaspoon sugar
1 tablespoon Chicken Stock, preferably salt-free (see pp. 76–77)
1 teaspoon Hot Sauce (see pp. 10–11)

1 cup peanut oil
¼ cup minced Pickled Ginger (see pp. 134–35)
2 whole scallions, cut into ⅛-inch rounds
1 teaspoon minced garlic
½ cup triangle-cut red sweet pepper
½ cup snow peas, strung and slant-cut
½ cup fresh water chestnuts, sliced into rounds
2 teaspoons Oriental sesame oil

1. Rinse the scallops, then drain in a strainer set over a bowl for about 15 minutes. Place the drained scallops on several layers of paper towels. Remove any particles of sand or shell. Change the scallops to fresh paper towels. Quarter the scallops if large.

2. Make the marinade by dissolving the 1 tablespoon water chestnut powder in the 1 tablespoon sherry, then adding the egg white. Stir until well combined. Add the scallops to the marinade and stir until they are coated. Place the scallops in the refrigerator and marinate for at least 1 hour or up to 12 hours.

3. Make the seasoning sauce by first dissolving the 1 teaspoon water chestnut powder in the 2 tablespoons sherry, then adding the dark and light soy sauce, vinegar, sugar, chicken stock, and Hot Sauce. Stir until well combined.

4. Place a wok over high heat for about 1 minute. Add the peanut oil and heat until it reaches 325°. Restir the scallops in the marinade and add half of them to the wok. Stir slowly with a pair of long cooking chopsticks in a circular motion for about 1 minute or until the scallops turn white. Remove the scallops with a wire strainer to a colander set over a bowl. Reheat the oil until it reaches 325° or until you can no longer hear the oil splattering. Add the other half of the scallops and repeat the cooking procedure. Transfer the scallops to the colander set over the bowl.

5. Do not wash the wok. Return any brown bits that have been caught in the sieve to the wok. Turn the heat to high and in the oil that glazes the wok, stir-fry the Pickled Ginger, scallions, garlic, and peppers for 1 minute. Add the snow peas and water chestnuts; continue to stir-fry 1 more minute. Restir the seasoning sauce and add it to the wok all at once. Stir about 30 seconds. Return the scallops to the wok. Continue to stir-fry until all the scallops have been evenly glazed with the sauce. Turn off the heat. Add the sesame oil. Mix a few seconds. Empty the contents of the wok onto a serving platter and serve immediately.

For the scallops you can substitute shrimp or boneless, skinless chicken breasts.

SERVES 2 to 3

Stir-Fried Shrimp Noodles with Lump Crabmeat

I love to serve this dish as a first course for a special occasion. It is my adaptation of a recipe Virginia Lee invented. A most innovative and amazing cook, she had the idea of making noodles with a base of shrimp instead of flour.

Once when I was making this dish for a class in Norfolk, Virginia, a student said, "This is delicious, I can't wait to try it with fresh crab." I said, "This is fresh crab." She said, "For me, fresh crab is when I catch, steam, and pick them myself." That's my kind of student.

½ cup dried Chinese mushrooms
¼ cup reduced mushroom stock (see step 1)
1 recipe Shrimp Noodles (see pp. 182–183)
1 cup reduced liquid from Shrimp Noodles (see page 183)
1 pound fresh lump crabmeat
2 medium-size carrots
1 tablespoon water chestnut powder
3 tablespoons peanut oil
1 teaspoon minced garlic
3 cups shredded bok choy, white and green parts included
1 teaspoon salt (optional)
2 tablespoons minced coriander leaves
1 whole scallion, minced

1. Rinse the mushrooms under cold running water. In a small bowl, soak them in cold water to cover for about 1 hour or until soft. Squeeze them over the bowl. Remove the stems and shred the mushrooms. Place the stems in a saucepan. Add the mushroom liquid. Reduce until about ¼ cup remains. Strain the mushroom stock then allow it to cool. Discard the stems.

2. Make the Shrimp Noodles, reserving 1 cup of the reduced liquid.

3. Pick over the crabmeat to remove all traces of shell and cartilage.

4. Slice the carrots. Blanch them for 3 minutes, then drain. Pass them through a food mill and reserve.

5. Make a binder by dissolving the water chestnut powder in the mushroom stock.

6. Place a wok over high heat for about 1 minute or until it smokes. Add the peanut oil. Turn the heat to low, then add the garlic. Stir a few seconds. Add the mushrooms, bok choy, and optional salt; stir-fry 1 minute over high heat. Add the crabmeat and gently toss another 30 seconds.

7. Pour reduced liquid from the Shrimp Noodles around the sides of the wok. Bring to a boil, then add the Shrimp Noodles.

8. Restir the binder and add it with one hand while stir-frying with the other. Taste for salt, adding more if necessary. Cook, stirring and tossing for about 1 minute. Slide the mixture onto a flat serving dish and sprinkle with coriander leaves and scallions. Dot the top of the dish with the pureed carrot, which resembles crab roe. Serve immediately.

This dish can be prepared ahead through step 5.

SERVES 4 to 6

Shrimp Noodles

These fascinating noodles are meant for Stir-fried Shrimp Noodles with Lump Crabmeat but are also marvelous in a clear chicken broth or as an addition to Chicken Vegetable Soup.

     1 pound medium shrimp (21–25 to the pound)
     5 tablespoons milk
     2 egg whites
     2 tablespoons medium-dry sherry
  1½ teaspoons salt
        Freshly ground white pepper (20 turns of the mill)
     5 tablespoons water chestnut powder
  One 1-inch chunk ginger
  1⅓ cups Chicken Stock, preferably salt-free (see pp. 76–77)
     2 whole scallions, cut into ⅛-inch rounds

SPECIAL EQUIPMENT
Pastry Bag
Number 48 pastry tube

1. Shell, devein, rinse, drain, and dry the shrimp on paper towels.

2. Place the milk, egg whites, sherry, salt, pepper, and water chestnut powder in the bowl of a food processor with a steel blade. Process the mixture using the on-and-off technique until well combined.

3. Cut the ginger in half (peeling is not necessary), then place it in a garlic press. Extract the juice into the processor bowl.

4. Add the shrimp to the processor and pulse until the mixture is smooth. Scrape the sides of the bowl if necessary from time to time to incorporate the mixture into a smooth paste. It should move freely in the processor bowl. If it is too stiff, add another tablespoon of sherry.

5. Place 1 quart of water in a saucepan. Pour in the chicken stock. Bring to a boil. Add the scallions and simmer 5 minutes. Remove the scallions and set them aside. Turn the heat to low but keep the stock simmering uncovered.

6. *To Make the Noodles:* Spoon the shrimp paste into a pastry bag that has been fitted with a number 48 pastry tube. This will make the noodles resemble the shape of thick fettucine. Squeeze the shrimp mixture into the simmering liquid in a circular motion. Keep the heat on low. The idea is to heat the noodles just until they set, without excessive cooking. Using a wire strainer, remove the shrimp noodles from the water and place them in a colander to drain.

7. Return the cooked scallions to the liquid in which the shrimp noodles were cooked, and reduce the liquid to about 1 cup. Discard the scallions. Reserve the reduced shrimp stock and the noodles for Stir-fried Shrimp Noodles with Lump Crabmeat.

Shrimp Noodles can be used immediately after cooking or stored, covered, for 1 day in the refrigerator.

YIELDS 1 pound Shrimp Noodles

Eastern Jambalaya

A perfect selection when entertaining, this delicious jam-balaya is a Chinese rendition of a Louisiana classic. Complete the meal with a salad, such as Jicama and Dandelion Salad.

2 cups Chicken Stock, preferably salt-free (see pp. 76–77)
½ teaspoon saffron
2 cups raw short-grain Japanese rice, preferably Kokuho Rose
1½ pounds chicken, including skin and bone, cut into bite size pieces

1 live lobster, weighing 2 pounds
1 pound medium shrimp (21–25 to the pound)

SEASONING SAUCE
2 tablespoons dark soy sauce
2 tablespoons oyster sauce
2 teaspoons Hot Sauce (see pp. 10–11)
½ cup Tomato Sauce (see pp. 16–17)

2 tablespoons olive oil
1 link smoked sausage, weighing 6 ounces, cut into ⅛-inch rounds
½ cup smoked ham, cut into 1-inch pieces
1 cup chopped Spanish onion
¾ cup chopped sweet peppers (combination of red and yellow)
2 teaspoons minced garlic
1¼ cups chopped well-ripened tomatoes
½ cup sliced (⅛-inch rounds) scallions, white and green parts included
1¼ cups chopped bok choy, white and green parts included

1. Bring the chicken stock to a simmer in a small saucepan. Add the saffron, turn off the heat, and let steep for 1 hour or longer, uncovered.

2. Preheat the oven to 350°.

3. Place the rice in a strainer; rinse under cold running water, then drain.

4. Rinse the chicken pieces, then dry on paper towels.

5. Using a heavy cleaver and rubber mallet, sever the spinal column of the lobster near the head almost all the way through. This will kill the lobster instantly. Chop the body of the lobster into 2-inch sections. Crack the claws. Remove the brain from the head and discard. Place the lobster pieces on a plate. If the lobster is female, include the roe and tomalley.

6. Shell, split, devein, rinse, drain, and dry the shrimp on paper towels.

7. Make the seasoning sauce by mixing together the soy sauce, oyster sauce, Hot Sauce, and Tomato Sauce. Stir until well combined.

8. Place a 5-quart heavy casserole with a tight-fitting cover over high heat for about 1 minute. Throughout step 8, keep the heat on high. Add the olive oil, then the sausage rounds; sauté 3 minutes, stirring occasionally. If the oil splatters, cover from time to time. Add the chicken pieces; sauté 2 minutes. Add the ham; sauté 3 minutes. Add the onion and continue to sauté for 2 minutes, stirring occasionally. Add the red and yellow peppers; sauté 1 minute. Add the garlic and stir a few seconds. Add the tomatoes; stir 1 minute. Add the scallions and the bok choy, stirring about 30 seconds. Add the drained rice and stir well another minute. Pour in the saffron stock and bring to a simmer. Add the seasoning sauce and stir well. Turn off the heat.

9. Cover the casserole, then place it in the preheated oven and bake for 15 minutes.

10. Remove the dish from the oven and add the lobster. Toss well to distribute the pieces. Cover and return the casserole to the oven for 3 minutes.

11. Remove the dish from the oven and mix in the shrimp. Cover and return the casserole to the oven for an additional 6

minutes. The total baking time is 24 minutes. Remove the casserole from the oven and serve immediately.

If desired, you can prepare the dish in advance through step 9. Remove the casserole from the oven and after 15 minutes, let the cover be askew. This procedure can be done several hours in advance. Before adding the seafood, rewarm the casserole for 10 minutes in a preheated oven.

For the Japanese rice, you can substitute long-grain rice, in which case you should increase the chicken stock to 2½ cups.

SERVES 6

Steamed Lobster with
Black Bean Ginger Mayonnaise

This variation on the typical herbed mayonnaise frequently chosen to accompany a poached or steamed lobster is a perfect choice for a summer lunch or evening meal.

2 live 1¼-pound lobsters

BLACK BEAN GINGER MAYONNAISE
⅓ cup mayonnaise
1 teaspoon minced fermented black beans
1 teaspoon minced Pickled Ginger (see pp. 134–135)
1 teaspoon Spicy Mustard Sauce (see page 14)
1 tablespoon lemon juice
1 tablespoon heavy cream

2 large arugula leaves

GARNISH
Chicory leaves

1. Bring 1 inch of water to a rolling boil in a casserole with a tight-fitting cover. Place the lobsters in the boiling water. Cover and cook over high heat for 2 minutes or until the water comes to a boil again. Turn the heat to medium low and simmer the lobsters another 8 minutes. Remove them from the casserole and allow to cool. Refrigerate the lobsters if you are not using them in the next hour.

2. Make the Black Bean Ginger Mayonnaise by mixing together the mayonnaise, black beans, Pickled Ginger, Spicy Mustard Sauce, lemon juice, and cream. Stir until well combined.

3. When ready to serve, split the lobsters in half. Crack the claws in a few places. Create a pocket in the head by removing the brain. Line the pocket with the arugula leaf and pour in the dressing. Place the lobsters on a plate. Garnish with chicory, then serve.

Steamed Lobster with Black Bean Ginger Mayonnaise can be prepared ahead through step 2.

SERVES 2

Soft-shell Crabs in Garlic Sauce

Soft-shell crabs are an American seasonal favorite. They are especially exciting with a Chinese seasoning sauce and sautéed scallions, ginger, and garlic. Your guests will never suspect it only took a few minutes to prepare.

1 pound small live soft-shell crabs (7 or 8 to the pound)
¼ cup flour for dredging

SEASONING SAUCE
2 tablespoons medium-dry sherry
1 teaspoon light soy sauce
1 tablespoon dark soy sauce
2 teaspoons sugar
2 teaspoons red wine vinegar
1 teaspoon Hot Sauce (see pp. 10–11)

4 tablespoons peanut oil
2 whole scallions, cut into ⅛-inch rounds
1 tablespoon minced garlic
1 teaspoon minced ginger
⅓ cup Chicken Stock, preferably salt-free (see pp. 76–77)

GARNISH
Lemon twists (see illustration, page 169)

1. For minimal loss of juices and maximum flavor, it is best to clean the crabs immediately before cooking; however, if you prefer the fishmonger to do it, it can be done several hours before cooking.

2. *To Clean the Crabs:* In order not to lose the juices, rinse the crab under cold running water before cleaning. Cut off the head with scissors or poultry shears. Using your fingers, take out the sac lodged behind the eyes. Turn the crab over and twist off the apron that folds under the rear of the body. Lift the soft cara-

pace (shell) and remove the feathery lungs. Leave the crabs whole. Place them on several layers of paper towels; then place more paper towels on top of the crabs. After 10 minutes, flip them over to dry the other side. If the crabs are still wet, repeat the drying procedure.

3. Dredge each crab with flour and shake off the excess.

4. Make the seasoning sauce by combining the sherry, light and dark soy sauce, sugar, vinegar, and Hot Sauce.

5. Preheat the oven to 250°.

6. Place a 14-inch skillet over high heat. Add 3 of the tablespoons of oil and heat until hot but not smoking. Place the crabs in the skillet in a single layer, shell-side down. Sauté the crabs over medium heat for about 2 minutes on each side. Shake the skillet occasionally. Transfer the crabs from the skillet to a flat oval-shaped serving dish. Keep them warm in the oven, uncovered.

7. Add the remaining 1 tablespoon of oil to the skillet. Sauté the scallions, garlic, and ginger over medium heat for about 1 minute. Pour in the stock. Turn the heat to high. Bring the stock to a boil and simmer for 1 minute.

8. Restir the seasoning sauce and add it to the skillet all at once, stirring until the sauce thickens slightly. Remove the crabs from the oven, then pour the sauce over them. Garnish with lemon twists.

SERVES 3

Soft-shell Crabs with Scallions and Pickled Ginger

An American crustacean, a French cooking technique, and Chinese seasonings blend here to form a speedy, succulent dish.

1 pound small live soft-shell crabs (7 or 8 to the pound)
¼ cup flour for dredging

SEASONING SAUCE
2 tablespoons medium-dry sherry
½ tablespoon light soy sauce
½ tablespoon dark soy sauce
1 teaspoon balsamic vinegar
1 teaspoon sugar

4 tablespoons peanut oil
⅓ cup finely shredded Pickled Ginger (see pp. 134–135)
1 cup shredded scallions, white and green parts included, split and cut into 3-inch lengths
1 teaspoon minced garlic
¼ cup Chicken Stock, preferably salt-free (see pp. 76–77)
1 teaspoon Oriental sesame oil

GARNISH
Lemon twists (see illustration, page 169)

1. For minimal loss of juices and maximum flavor, it is best to clean the crabs immediately before cooking; however, if you prefer the fishmonger to do it, it can be done several hours before cooking.

2. *To Clean the Crabs*: In order not to lose the juices, rinse the crab under cold running water before cleaning. Cut off the head with scissors or poultry shears. Using your fingers, take out

the sac lodged behind the eyes. Turn the crab over and twist off the apron that folds under the rear of the body. Lift the soft carapace (shell) and remove the feathery lungs. Leave the crabs whole. Place them on several layers of paper towels; then place more paper towels on top of the crabs. After 10 minutes, flip them over to dry the other side. If the crabs are still wet, repeat the drying procedure.

3. Dredge each crab in flour and shake off the excess.

4. Make the seasoning sauce by combining the sherry, light and dark soy sauce, vinegar, and sugar.

5. Preheat the oven to 250°.

6. Place a 14-inch skillet over high heat. Add 3 of the tablespoons of peanut oil and heat until hot but not smoking. Place the crabs in the skillet in a single layer, shell-side down. Sauté the crabs over medium heat for about 2 minutes on each side. Shake the skillet occasionally. Transfer the crabs from the skillet to a flat oval-shaped serving dish. Keep them warm in the oven, uncovered.

7. Add the remaining 1 tablespoon of peanut oil to the skillet. Add the Pickled Ginger and scallions. Sauté over high heat for about 30 seconds. Add the garlic; stir-fry another 30 seconds.

8. Restir the seasoning sauce, then add it to the skillet, stirring about 30 seconds or until the sauce thickens. Add the stock and simmer another 30 seconds, stirring all the while. Turn off the heat. Add the sesame oil. Stir briefly.

9. Remove the crabs from the oven and pour the sauce over them. Garnish with lemon twists.

SERVES 3

Lobster with Scallions and Pickled Ginger

This variation on Soft-shell Crabs with Scallions and Pickled Ginger works beautifully with a live lobster when soft-shell crabs are not in season or if lobster is a preference.

1 live female lobster, weighing 1½ pounds
½ cup combined lobster juice (see step 1) and Chicken Stock, preferably salt-free (see pp. 76–77)

SEASONING SAUCE
1 teaspoon water chestnut powder
2 tablespoons medium-dry sherry
½ tablespoon dark soy sauce
½ tablespoon light soy sauce
1 teaspoon balsamic vinegar
1 teaspoon sugar

2 tablespoons peanut oil
⅓ cup finely shredded Pickled Ginger (see pp. 134–135)
1 cup shredded scallions, white and green parts included
1 teaspoon minced garlic
1 teaspoon Oriental sesame oil

1. Using a heavy cleaver and rubber mallet, sever the spinal column of the lobster near the head almost all the way through. This will kill the lobster instantly. Chop the body of the lobster into 2-inch sections. Crack the claws. Remove the brain from the head and discard. Place the lobster pieces in a strainer set over a 4-cup Pyrex measuring cup. Collect the drained juices. Add the roe and tomalley (the liver). Pour in enough chicken stock to yield ½ cup. Set this stock mixture aside.

2. Make the seasoning sauce by dissolving the water chestnut powder in the sherry and then adding the dark soy sauce, light soy sauce, vinegar, and sugar. Combine in a small bowl.

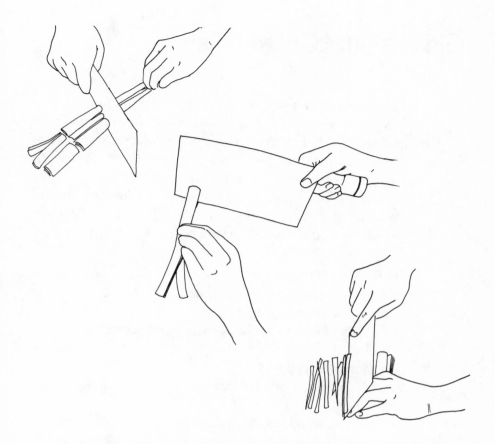

3. Place a wok over high heat for about 1 minute or until it smokes. Add the peanut oil and heat a few seconds. Add the Pickled Ginger and the scallions; stir-fry about 30 seconds. Add the garlic and stir-fry for another 30 seconds. Add the lobster pieces and stir-fry 2 minutes. Add the stock mixture; cover, then turn the heat to medium. Cook approximately 4 minutes or until the shells turn intensely red.

4. Remove the cover, turn the heat to high. Restir the seasoning sauce and add it all at once to the wok; stir-fry about 30 more seconds or until the sauce thickens. Turn off the heat and add the sesame oil, mix a few seconds, then empty the contents of the wok onto a flat white serving platter. Serve immediately.

SERVES 2

Ginger Butter Grilled Lobster

The Chinese don't have the luxury of a broiler in their homes, so when they cook a lobster they have to cut it up and stir-fry it. For this recipe I have taken just a hint of Chinese seasonings and combined it with the American technique of broiling. Lobster prepared this way preserves its true flavor so that those who only eat lobster steamed with drawn butter can also enjoy this dish. A good accompaniment would be Pasta with Fresh Wild Mushrooms.

SEASONED BUTTER
3 tablespoons sweet butter, softened
1 tablespoon minced ginger
½ cup finely chopped scallions, white and green parts
    included
1½ teaspoons minced garlic
    Freshly ground white pepper (15 turns of the mill)

1 live lobster, weighing 1½-pounds
½ lemon

1. Preheat the oven to broil.
2. Make the seasoned butter by kneading together the butter, ginger, scallions, garlic, and pepper with the heel of your hand.
3. Lay the lobster, stomach-side down, on a chopping block. Sever the spinal column by inserting a cleaver or knife through the back of the shell where the tail and the body sections meet. Lay the lobster on its back. Using a pair of scissors, cut the undershell down the middle. Then using a heavy cleaver and rubber mallet, split the lobster in half, starting from the head and going down to the tail. Remove the brain, which is in the form of a sac located near the eyes. Also remove the intestinal tract, which is located in the tail section. Do not remove the roe or tomalley (liver). Crack the claws almost all the way through by placing a

paper towel in between the cleaver and the lobster claw. Use a heavy cleaver and rubber mallet for the procedure.

4. Place the lobster on an oval-shaped heat-proof dish that is suitable to bring to the table. Squeeze the juice of the lemon over the lobster. Spread the seasoned butter over the meat (not the claws). Broil the lobster for 10 minutes, 4 inches from the heat source. Serve immediately.

SERVES 1 to 2

Tea Smoked Lobster with Lemon Caper Sauce

I have substituted lobster for duck in this variation on the classic Tea Smoked Duck from Sichuan Province. Tea Smoked Lobster is a much speedier dish than the traditional one, as the duck needs to be marinated, steamed, smoked, and then deep-fried. Served hot or room temperature, Tea Smoked Lobster makes an impressive appetizer for 4 to 6 guests or an entrée for 2 to 3.

  1 live lobster, weighing 3 pounds
  1 cup raw short-grain brown rice
  ½ cup brown sugar
  ½ cup Lapsang Souchong tea leaves

  LEMON CAPER SAUCE
  4 tablespoons butter
 1½ tablespoons minced shallots
 1½ tablespoons capers, rinsed
  2 teaspoons lemon juice
 1½ tablespoons dry white wine

1. Bring 1 inch of water to a rolling boil in a casserole with a tight-fitting cover. Place the lobster in the boiling water, cover, and cook over high heat for 2 minutes or until the lobster turns red. Remove the lobster from the casserole to a platter.

2. Line a wok with heavy-duty aluminum foil. In a bowl, combine the rice, sugar, and tea leaves. Empty this mixture into the wok and spread slightly. Shorten 4 chopsticks by cutting, then breaking off about 2 inches of 1 end. Arrange 2 of the shortened chopsticks parallel to each other and about 2 inches apart on top of the rice mixture; then place 2 more chopsticks on top of these in the opposite direction to form a tic-tac-toe pattern. Place the lobster on the chopsticks. Line a wok cover with aluminum foil,

extending the foil a few inches beyond the rim. Put the cover on the wok. It should fit tightly.

3. Turn the heat to medium low. Smoke the lobster for 30 minutes without lifting the lid. Turn off the heat but leave the covered wok on the burner for another 30 minutes. (If using an electric stove, remove from the heat source.) Remove the lobster from the wok and let it cool for 5 minutes.

4. While the lobster is cooling, prepare the Lemon Caper Sauce: In a small skillet melt 3 tablespoons of the butter over low heat. Add the shallots and sauté for 2 minutes or until they soften. While the shallots are sautéing, crush the capers with the side of a cleaver. Add the lemon juice and white wine to the skillet. Stir about 2 minutes, still over low heat. Add the capers. Sauté another minute. Add the remaining 1 tablespoon of butter. Stir briefly until it melts and thickens the sauce. Turn off the heat.

5. Split the tail of the lobster in half, then remove the intestinal tract. Spoon a tablespoon or more of the Lemon Caper Sauce over the tail. Place the remaining sauce in a ramekin and serve the lobster with the sauce on the side.

A large lobster is required for this technique, as it is necessary for the lobster to stay in the smoker for 1 hour in order to acquire a smoky flavor. A small lobster would be overcooked.

Tea Smoked Lobster with Lemon Caper Sauce can be prepared several hours in advance. Do not refrigerate.

SERVES 2 to 6

Chinese Lobster Fra Diavolo

*This Chinese version of the classic Italian Lobster Fra Dia-
volo is very fast to prepare, assuming you have some homemade Tomato Sauce and Hot Sauce on hand. Rice, pasta,
or bread is a must for this dish in order to soak up the good
sauce.*

1 live lobster, weighing 1¼ to 1½-pounds

SEASONING SAUCE
½ cup Tomato Sauce (see pp. 16–17)
1 teaspoon Hot Sauce (see pp. 10–11)
1 teaspoon dark soy sauce
2 tablespoons Chicken Stock, preferably salt-free (see
    pp. 76–77)

2 tablespoons peanut oil
¼ cup chopped onion
2 teaspoons minced garlic
2 whole scallions, cut into ⅛-inch rounds
1 teaspoon minced ginger
¼ cup medium-dry sherry
2 tablespoons cognac

1. Using a heavy cleaver and rubber mallet, sever the spinal
column of the lobster near the head almost all the way through.
This will kill the lobster instantly. Chop the body of the lobster
into 2-inch sections. Crack the claws. Remove the brain from the
head and discard. Place the lobster pieces in a strainer set over a
bowl; collect the drained juices. Add the lobster roe (if female) and
the tomalley (liver) to the collected lobster juices.

2. Make the seasoning sauce by mixing together the Tomato
Sauce, Hot Sauce, soy sauce, and chicken stock. Stir until well
combined.

3. Place a wok over high heat for about 1 minute or until it

smokes. Add the peanut oil and heat a few seconds. Add the lobster pieces and stir-fry 2 minutes.

4. Add the onion, garlic, scallions, and ginger; stir-fry about 1 minute.

5. Add the sherry and allow to reduce about 30 seconds. Add the cognac; reduce a few seconds. Pour in the seasoning sauce. Cover, turn the heat to medium and cook for 5 minutes. Remove the cover and turn the heat to high. Cook for a few seconds or until the sauce has thickened. Empty the contents of the wok onto a heated serving dish and serve immediately.

SERVES 2

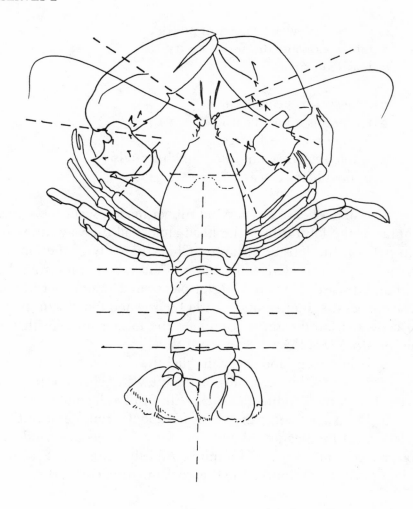

Lobster Cantonese with Caviar

This interesting twist on an old Cantonese classic uses caviar as a substitute for the traditional pork and salted black beans.

1 live female lobster, weighing 1¼ to 1½ pounds
½ cup Chicken Stock (see pp. 76–77)
1 whole egg, plus 1 egg white

BINDER
½ tablespoon water chestnut powder
3 tablespoons medium-dry sherry
½ teaspoon sugar

2 tablespoons peanut oil
2 teaspoons minced garlic
1 teaspoon minced ginger
2 whole scallions, cut into ⅛-inch rounds
2 ounces black caviar

1. Using a heavy cleaver and rubber mallet, sever the spinal column of the lobster near the head almost all the way through. This will kill the lobster instantly. Chop the body of the lobster into 2-inch sections. Crack the claws. Remove the brain from the head and discard. Place the lobster pieces in a strainer set over a bowl; collect the drained juices. Add the roe and tomally (liver) to the collected lobster juices. Combine the lobster juices with the chicken stock. Set this stock mixture aside.
2. Beat the egg and egg white slightly.
3. Make the binder by dissolving the water chestnut powder in the sherry, then adding the sugar. Stir until well combined.
4. Place a wok over high heat for about 1 minute or until it smokes. Add the peanut oil and heat for a few seconds. Add the lobster pieces and stir-fry 2 minutes. Add the garlic, ginger, and scallions; stir-fry 1 minute. Add the stock mixture, cover, then turn

the heat to medium. Cook approximately 4 minutes or until the shells turn intensely red. Remove the cover. Turn the heat to high. Restir the binder and add it to the wok all at once; stir-fry about 30 seconds or until the sauce thickens. Stir in the eggs and immediately turn off the heat.

5. Arrange the lobster pieces on a serving dish to resemble the shape of a whole lobster. Place the caviar on top and serve immediately.

SERVES 2

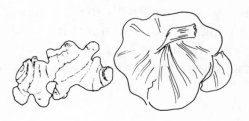

Shad Roe and Asparagus with Ginger Butter Sauce

This dish, which pairs two American ingredients with Chinese seasonings, is for those of you who can't wait for spring because it is the time of year when both shad roe and asparagus are at the height of their season.

1 pair shad roe, weighing approximately 1 pound
3 tablespoons sweet butter, at room temperature
1 pound asparagus
2 tablespoons minced shallots
1 teaspoon minced ginger
4 tablespoons medium-dry sherry
1 teaspoon dark soy sauce

1. Preheat the oven to broil. Spread 1 tablespoon of the butter over the shad roe and broil for 8 to 10 minutes.
2. To determine the tender portion of the asparagus, hold the bottom of each individual stalk in the left hand, in a gently closed fist. With the right hand, palm open, slap the green stalk so that it breaks cleanly. Make one slant cut on each asparagus end. Steam the asparagus for about 5 minutes or until they are tender.
3. Heat the remaining 2 tablespoons of butter in a small skillet and sauté the shallots for 2 minutes over low heat. Add the ginger and sauté another minute. Add 1 tablespoon of the sherry and the soy sauce; stir briefly. Turn off the heat.
4. Remove the shad roe from the broiler and transfer it to an oval-shaped serving platter. Deglaze the pan in which the shad roe was broiled with the remaining 3 tablespoons of sherry by placing the pan over direct heat. Add these deglazed juices to the ginger-butter sauce. Surround the shad roe with the steamed asparagus and spoon the sauce over both.

SERVES 2

Poultry

CANTONESE FRIED CHICKEN

COQ AU SHERRY

SAUTÉED CHICKEN BREASTS
WITH ORANGE SAUCE

SHOEMAKER CHICKEN

CHICKEN WITH RED GINGER BARBECUE SAUCE

STUFFED CHICKEN BREASTS WITH
GINGER MIRIN SAUCE

BARBECUED ROAST CHICKEN

CHICKEN CURRY

PEKING TURKEY

DEEP-FRIED MARINATED QUAIL

BRAISED ROCK CORNISH HENS
IN OYSTER SAUCE

SHERRY MUSTARD ROASTED
ROCK CORNISH HENS

Cantonese Fried Chicken

This chicken recipe is totally addictive. Once you try the twice-frying Chinese cooking technique on chicken, you may never go back to your traditional method. Twice-frying follows the same principle as the French Pommes Frites: once for the cooking and then again for the texture. This technique allows the chicken to remain crisp even after it has cooled. For that reason you may serve Cantonese Fried Chicken hot or at room temperature.

1   chicken, weighing 4 to 5 pounds, cut into approximately
     1½-inch pieces

     MARINADE
One   1-inch chunk ginger
  4   whole scallions, cut into 1-inch lengths
  ⅓   cup light soy sauce
  ¼   cup medium-dry sherry
1½   tablespoons Oriental sesame oil
  2   teaspoons sugar
     Freshly ground black pepper (25 turns of the mill)

1   box (½ pound) lumpy water chestnut powder for
     dredging

4   cups peanut oil for deep-frying

     GARNISH
1   bunch watercress, 2 inches of stems removed

Sichuan Peppercorn Powder (see page 13) for dipping

1. Rinse the chicken under cold running water. Drain and dry well with paper towels.

2. Cut the ginger in half (peeling is not necessary), then place it in a garlic press. Extract the juice over a bowl large enough to hold the chicken and the marinade.

3. Add the scallions, soy sauce, sherry, sesame oil, sugar, and pepper to the bowl. Stir until the marinade is well combined. Add the chicken to the bowl, tossing well. Allow it to marinate in the refrigerator for at least 4 hours, but not more than 6 hours (because the chicken gets too salty). Turn the chicken occasionally in the marinade. Remove the chicken from the refrigerator 30 minutes before frying.

4. Drain the chicken from the marinade, then dredge each piece, one at a time, in the water chestnut powder. If the skin has separated from the chicken, replace the skin before the chicken comes in contact with the water chestnut powder.

5. Place a wok over high heat for about 1 minute or until it smokes. Pour in the oil and heat until the oil reaches 350°. If you don't have a deep-fat frying thermometer, you can stand a chopstick upright in the middle of the wok; the oil is ready when bubbles form rapidly around the chopstick. Add the chicken pieces, not more than 8 to 10 at a time. Cook for about 5 minutes, turning the pieces in the oil occasionally. Remove the chicken with a wire strainer: drain it well on several sheets of paper towels. Reheat the oil before adding another batch of chicken. The oil is ready to receive more chicken when you can no longer hear the bubbles popping. Reheating the oil after every batch of chicken is extremely important, lest the chicken become soggy because the oil is not hot enough. Repeat the frying process until all the pieces have been fried once and drained on paper towels. Let the chicken and the oil cool at least 30 minutes (up to 4 hours).

6. Reheat the oil to 375°. Add the chicken pieces, no more than 6 at a time. Fry about 30 seconds or until the chicken turns golden brown. Add another batch of chicken and repeat the frying process until all the chicken pieces have been fried twice and drained on paper towels.

7. Serve Cantonese Fried Chicken hot or at room temperature. Garnish with watercress. Each diner places a little Sichuan Peppercorn Powder on her plate to use for dipping the chicken.

There are 2 types of water chestnut powder; a coarse-textured variety and a smooth one. Try to find the coarse-grain texture for this recipe as the exterior of the chicken will be more crunchy.

I like to marinate the chicken in an oval-shaped dish with a lip because it sits in the marinade better.

SERVES 4 to 6

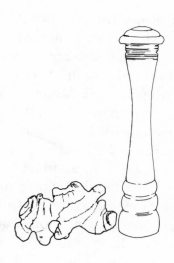

Coq Au Sherry

This is a Chinese bistro dish, a variation of the classic French Coq au Vin.

¼ cup dried Chinese mushrooms
1 tablespoon reduced mushroom stock (see step 1)
1 chicken, weighing 2½ to 3 pounds, cut into eighths
¾ cup small shallots
¾ cup bacon, cut into 1-inch-long by ¼-inch-wide pieces
1 cup dry sherry
¼ cup cognac
¼ cup Chicken Stock, preferably salt-free (see pp. 76–77)
½ teaspoon five spice powder
½ teaspoon salt
  Freshly ground black pepper (10 turns of the mill)

  BEURRE MANIÉ
1 tablespoon sweet butter
1 teaspoon water chestnut powder

1. Rinse the mushrooms under cold running water. In a small bowl, soak them in cold water to cover for about 1 hour or until soft. Squeeze them over the bowl. Remove the stems and quarter the mushrooms. Set the mushrooms aside. Place the stems in a saucepan. Add the mushroom liquid. Reduce until about 1 tablespoon remains. Strain the mushroom stock and reserve. Discard the stems.

2. Rinse the chicken parts under cold running water. Drain and dry well with paper towels.

3. Place the shallots in a strainer and pour boiling water over them to loosen the skins. Peel and leave them whole.

4. Place a 10-inch skillet over high heat for about 1 minute. Add the bacon, then turn the heat to low and sauté about 3 minutes or until the bacon has lightly browned.

5. Remove the bacon and add the chicken, skin-side down. Sauté over medium heat for about 5 minutes or until one side is brown. Turn the chicken over and brown on the other side for another 5 minutes.

6. Tilt the skillet and remove the fat, except for 1 tablespoon. Add the shallots and sauté for 1 minute. Add the mushrooms, sherry, and cognac. Allow to reduce about 1 minute. Add the chicken stock and the mushroom stock; continue to reduce for another minute. Add the five spice powder, cooked bacon, salt, and pepper. Cover and simmer 10 minutes. Uncover and reduce another 3 minutes or until approximately ½ cup sauce remains.

7. Knead together the butter and water chestnut powder with the heel of your hand. Add this beurre manié to the simmering sauce. Stir until the sauce thickens. Serve immediately.

The entire dish can be prepared a day in advance and rewarmed in a covered casserole for 10 minutes in a preheated 350° oven.

SERVES 2

Sautéed Chicken Breasts with Orange Sauce

This rendition of Orange Chicken does not require cutting or marinating the chicken, which saves the cook much time and effort. It is also different from the classic dish in that my adaptation of a beurre manié is used to thicken the sauce instead of the traditional cornstarch-sherry binder. I have chosen this French method because I not only wanted to thicken the sauce but also to enrich it with the taste of butter, which is exactly the purpose of a beurre manié.

1 pound boneless, skinless chicken breasts

1 tablespoon flour for dredging

SEASONING SAUCE
1 tablespoon orange flavored liqueur
2 tablespoons white wine
½ tablespoon light soy sauce
1 tablespoon dark soy sauce
3 tablespoons Chicken Stock, preferably salt-free (see pp. 76–77)
½ tablespoon sugar
1 teaspoon Hot Sauce (see pp. 10–11)
1 teaspoon Chinese red vinegar
  Zest of 1 orange, grated
2 tablespoons fresh orange juice

BEURRE MANIÉ
1 tablespoon sweet butter
½ tablespoon water chestnut powder

3 tablespoons peanut oil
1 tablespoon sweet butter
½ cup diced red sweet pepper
3 whole scallions, cut into ⅛-inch rounds
2 teaspoons minced ginger
2 teaspoons minced garlic

1. Trim the chicken breasts to remove all traces of fat, cartilage, and membrane. Sprinkle them with flour.

2. Make the seasoning sauce by mixing together the liqueur, wine, light and dark soy sauce, chicken stock, sugar, Hot Sauce, vinegar, orange zest, and orange juice. Stir until well combined.

3. Make a beurre manié by kneading the 1 tablespoon butter and the water chestnut powder with the heel of your hand on a chopping block. Set aside.

4. Preheat the oven to 250°. Place a 12-inch skillet over high heat for about 1 minute. Add the peanut oil and heat until hot but not smoking. Add the chicken breasts to the skillet and sauté for 8 minutes, turning once at midpoint. Transfer the chicken breasts from the skillet to a heat-proof serving dish. Place the chicken in the preheated oven, uncovered.

5. Add the 1 tablespoon butter to the skillet. Turn the heat to low. As soon as the butter has melted, add the peppers, scallions, ginger, and garlic; sauté 1 minute. Restir the seasoning sauce and add it to the wok; turn the heat to high, stirring constantly. After the sauce has come to a boil, cook for 1 minute. Gradually (you may not need it all), add the beurre manié. Stir until the sauce has formed a thick, syrupy glaze. Turn off the heat. Pour the sauce over the chicken breasts and serve immediately.

This dish can be prepared in advance through step 3.

SERVES 2 to 3

Shoemaker Chicken

This is a Chinese version of the Italian dish called Chicken Scarpariello, literally translated as "in the style of the shoemaker." Deep-fried instead of sautéed, this chicken is seasoned with sherry and soy sauce instead of white wine or lemon and is accented with a surprising trace of fresh coriander and oyster mushrooms.

1 chicken, weighing 2 pounds, cut into 1½-inch pieces
    with the skin and bone
2 tablespoons water chestnut powder
1 teaspoon salt
    Freshly ground black pepper (15 turns of the mill)
¼ pound fresh oyster mushrooms
1 cup corn oil
1 cup triangle-cut red and yellow sweet peppers
1 tablespoon minced garlic
3 tablespoons chopped parsley
1 tablespoon chopped coriander leaves
1 tablespoon dark soy sauce
¼ cup medium-dry sherry

1. Rinse the chicken under cold running water. Drain and dry well with paper towels. Place the chicken in a bowl. Add the water chestnut powder, salt, and pepper. Toss to coat.

2. Clean the oyster mushrooms with a pastry or mushroom brush. Cut off and discard the hard part of the stems. Cut the remaining part of the stems crosswise thinly. Cut the mushrooms into thick strips, maintaining their shape. If small, leave whole.

3. Place a wok over high heat for about 1 minute or until it smokes. Pour in the corn oil and heat until it reaches 350°. If you don't have a deep-fat frying thermometer, you can stand a chopstick upright in the middle of the wok; the oil is ready when bubbles form rapidly around the chopstick. Add half the chicken and fry over high heat, stirring occasionally, for about 6 to 7 minutes

or until it is brown and crisp. Cover the wok if splattering. Remove the chicken from the wok with a wire strainer. Drain on paper towels. Reheat the oil to 350° and fry the remaining chicken for 6 to 7 minutes over high heat. Remove the second batch of chicken with a wire strainer and drain on paper towels. Turn off the heat. Pour the oil, except for 2 tablespoons, out of the wok through a strainer, then knock back the brown bits into the wok.

4. Turn the heat to high. To the 2 tablespoons oil, add the peppers; stir-fry 2 minutes. Add the mushrooms; stir-fry 1 minute. Add the garlic, parsley, and coriander; stir-fry about 30 seconds. Add the soy sauce and sherry; continue to stir-fry another 30 seconds. Return the chicken to the wok and stir briefly or until all the ingredients are well combined. Empty the contents of the wok into a serving dish and serve immediately.

Both the Italians and the Chinese frequently cut chicken into bite-size pieces before cooking for easy-eating, main-course dishes.

SERVES 2 to 3

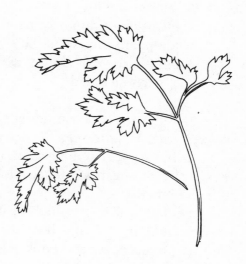

Chicken with Red Ginger Barbecue Sauce

This is the kind of dish I would make for a Fourth of July party. The chicken is fried crisp, with a Chinese-American barbecue sauce that glazes each piece.

1 chicken, weighing 3 pounds, cut into approximately 1½-inch pieces (reserve the legs for stock)

2 tablespoons flour for dredging

SEASONING SAUCE
5 tablespoons Tomato Sauce (see pp. 16–17)
3 tablespoons medium-dry sherry
3 tablespoons dark brown sugar
2 tablespoons dark soy sauce
1 tablespoon red wine vinegar
1 teaspoon Hot Sauce (see pp. 10–11)

⅓ cup peanut oil
1½ tablespoons minced ginger
2 teaspoons minced garlic
⅓ cup sliced (⅛-inch rounds) scallions, white and green parts included

1. Rinse the chicken under cold running water. Drain and dry well with paper towels. Dredge each piece lightly in the flour.

2. Make the seasoning sauce by mixing together the Tomato Sauce, sherry, sugar, soy sauce, vinegar, and Hot Sauce. Stir until well combined.

3. Place a wok over high heat for about 1 minute or until it smokes. Add the oil and heat for a few seconds. Add half the chicken pieces; cover and cook over high heat, turning occasionally, for about 6 to 7 minutes or until they are cooked through on

the inside and are crisp on the outside. Cover the wok if splattering. Remove the chicken from the wok with a wire strainer and place on a flat serving platter. Add the remaining chicken to the wok, continuing to cook over high heat for another 5 minutes. Turn the chicken pieces occasionally. Remove them from the wok with a wire strainer. Pour off the oil.

4. In the oil that glazes the wok, stir-fry the ginger, garlic and scallions about 1 minute. Restir the seasoning sauce and add it to the wok all at once, stirring for about 2 minutes over high heat until the sauce has reduced and thickened. Return the fried chicken pieces to the wok and stir 30 seconds or until the sauce has coated all the chicken pieces. Empty the contents of the wok onto a serving dish and serve immediately.

SERVES 3

Stuffed Chicken Breasts with Ginger Mirin Sauce

This recipe combines the Western techniques of stuffing and sautéing chicken breasts with an Eastern sauce.

STUFFING

3 tablespoons sweet butter
1½ tablespoons minced shallots
1 cup finely chopped bok choy, white and green parts included
½ teaspoon salt
Freshly ground black pepper (10 turns of the mill)
½ cup ricotta
⅓ cup diced mozzarella (3 ounces)
¼ cup pine nuts
1 egg yolk

3 whole chicken breasts, weighing approximately 14 ounces each

SEASONING SAUCE

2 tablespoons mirin sweet cooking rice wine
¾ tablespoon hoisin sauce
¾ tablespoon dark soy sauce

2 tablespoons flour for dredging
2 tablespoons olive oil
2 tablespoons corn oil
3 tablespoons minced Pickled Ginger (see pp. 134–135)

¼ cup medium-dry sherry
2 tablespoons Chicken Stock, preferably salt-free (see pp. 76–77)

SPECIAL EQUIPMENT
Unwaxed dental floss

1. Place a skillet over low heat. Add the butter and heat until melted. Add the shallots and cook about 2 minutes or until they have softened. Turn the heat to medium and add the bok choy, salt, and pepper. Sauté for 2 to 3 minutes or until the bok choy has wilted. Turn off the heat and set aside. Allow to reach room temperature.

2. In a bowl, combine the ricotta, mozzarella, pine nuts, and egg yolk. Add the vegetable mixture to the cheese mixture. Mix well and refrigerate for 1 hour.

3. While the stuffing is in the refrigerator, bone and skin the chicken breasts. Separate the fillet from each cutlet; you should have 6 halves. Trim each chicken breast carefully to remove all traces of fat, membrane, and cartilage. Cut a pocket into each cutlet by pressing your fingers on top of it while slicing into it until halved but not severed, almost as if it were butterflied.

4. Make the seasoning sauce by mixing together the mirin rice wine, hoisin sauce, and soy sauce.

5. Open the cutlet and, depending on the size of the breast, add approximately 2 tablespoons of the stuffing. Close the cutlet. In order for the stuffing to be covered completely, supplement the cutlet with a strip of fillet. Take unwaxed dental floss and tie the stuffed cutlet in at least 2 places. Refrigerate the chicken breast at least 2 hours or up to 12 hours.

6. Remove the chicken breasts from the refrigerator; do not allow to reach room temperature. Lightly flour the chicken breasts on all sides. Place a 12-inch skillet over high heat for about 1 minute. Add the olive oil and corn oil. Heat for a few seconds, then add the 6 chicken halves. Sauté for 3 to 4 minutes. Lower the heat if they are browning too fast. Shake the skillet occasionally to prevent them from sticking. Turn the chicken breasts over and sauté another 3 to 4 minutes. Remove the chicken breasts from the skillet to a flat serving platter.

7. Place the skillet over low heat. Add the Pickled Ginger and sauté 1 minute. Restir the seasoning sauce and add it to the skillet all at once, stirring a few seconds. Add the sherry and the

chicken stock. Continue to stir until the sauce forms a thick, syrupy glaze. Pour the sauce over the chicken breasts and serve immediately.

<hr>

Mirin Sweet Cooking Rice Wine can be purchased in Oriental markets as well as many supermarkets.

<hr>

SERVES 4 to 6

Barbecued Roast Chicken

The ancient Chinese method of air-drying the skin of poultry is really worth the extra trouble because the skin of the bird becomes parchment crisp and stays crisp even after the chicken has cooled to room temperature, which makes a dish that employs the technique a great option for a picnic.

1 chicken, weighing 3½ pounds

MARINADE
1 tablespoon dark soy sauce
1 tablespoon dry vermouth
1 tablespoon Oriental sesame oil
½ teaspoon five spice powder
1 teaspoon minced garlic

2 thin slices ginger
2 whole scallions
½ cup dry vermouth

1. Pull out the pockets of fat from the tail end of the chicken. Lift the flap of skin near the neck and remove any glands.

Place the chicken in the sink and pour about a gallon of boiling water over the outside skin.

2. *To Air-Dry the Chicken, Method 1, Outside:* If the temperature is between 35° and 45°, and it is a clear, windy day, hang the chicken outside for 8 to 24 hours or until the skin is dry and taut.

Method 2, Inside: Air-dry the chicken with a portable electric fan for 4 hours, 2 hours on the breast side, 2 hours on the back side. Another possibility is to air-dry it in the refrigerator by placing the chicken on a rack resting on a plate and changing the position of the chicken, breast-side up, breast-side down, every 12 hours. The chicken's skin should be dry after 24 hours.

3. When ready to roast the chicken, preheat the oven to 350°.

4. Make the marinade by mixing together the soy sauce, the 1 tablespoon vermouth, sesame oil, five spice powder, and garlic. Stir until well combined. Rub the marinade over the outside skin of the chicken for several minutes. Any excess marinade should be rubbed on the inside of the chicken.

5. Stuff the ginger slices and scallions into the cavity of the chicken.

6. Place the chicken on a high-legged rack that fits into a shallow roasting pan. Roast the chicken for 30 minutes breast-side down in the preheated oven. Add the ½ cup vermouth to the bottom of the roasting pan to prevent the juices from burning. Then turn the chicken breast-side up and roast for 20 minutes.

7. Turn the oven to 450° and roast for a final 10 minutes. Remove the chicken from the oven and allow it to cool for 10 minutes. Quarter and serve warm or at room temperature. If desired, make a natural sauce by first defatting, then deglazing the roasting-pan juices with a little stock; serve with this natural sauce.

Remember not to baste the chicken. Basting draws the juices out of the bird and prevents the skin from becoming crisp.

SERVES 4

Chicken Curry

Normally an Indian curry dish would call for a slow, long simmering, which produces a stewlike consistency. My Chicken Curry combines this traditional Indian spice with the Chinese technique of quick stir-frying, resulting in crisp vegetables and tender chicken.

1 pound boneless, skinless chicken breasts

MARINADE
1 tablespoon water chestnut powder
1 tablespoon medium-dry sherry
1 egg white
½ teaspoon salt
2 tablespoons curry powder

SEASONING SAUCE
1 tablespoon tomato paste
1 tablespoon dark soy sauce
2 teaspoons Hot Sauce (see pp. 10–11)

1 large Spanish onion
4 tablespoons peanut oil
1 cup triangle-cut red sweet peppers
2 teaspoons minced garlic
½ teaspoon salt
1 cup snow peas, strung and slant-cut in half once
2 tablespoons medium-dry sherry

1. Trim the chicken breasts to remove all traces of fat, cartilage, and membrane. Cut the chicken into ¾-inch cubes. Make the marinade by first dissolving the water chestnut powder in the 1 tablespoon sherry, then adding the egg white and ½ teaspoon salt. Add the chicken cubes and stir vigorously. Add the curry

powder and continue to stir until well combined. Place the mixture in the refrigerator for at least 1 hour or up to 12 hours.

2. Make the seasoning sauce by mixing together the tomato paste, soy sauce, and Hot Sauce. Stir until well combined.

3. Quarter, then cut the onion into 1-inch pieces. The yield should be 2½ cups cut onions.

4. Place a wok over high heat for about 1 minute or until it smokes. Add 2 tablespoons of the peanut oil and heat a few seconds. Add the onions and stir-fry about 2 minutes or until they begin to scorch. Add the peppers and continue to stir-fry 1½ minutes. Add the garlic and ½ teaspoon salt; continue to stir-fry a few seconds. Add the snow peas and stir-fry 30 seconds. Empty the contents of the wok onto a heated serving dish.

5. Return the wok to high heat. Add the remaining 2 tablespoons of peanut oil and heat a few seconds. Restir the chicken in the marinade and add it to the wok all at once. Stir-fry the chicken for about 2 minutes or until it becomes white.

6. Add the seasoning sauce and continue to stir-fry another 30 seconds. Add the 2 tablespoons of sherry around the sides of the wok; stir-fry a few seconds. Return the vegetables to the wok and continue to stir-fry another few seconds or until all the ingredients have been well combined. Empty the contents of the wok onto a heated serving dish and serve immediately.

Chicken Curry can be prepared early in the day through step 3.

SERVES 2 to 3

Peking Turkey

This is how I prepare turkey for my family on Thanksgiving. I have adapted the technique the Chinese use for Peking duck, only I do not separate the skin from the meat or defat the turkey since this bird needs every bit of natural fat it has. The secret to a juicy bird is not to overcook it and not to baste it. Basting draws the juices out of the bird and prevents the skin from becoming crisp. Any stuffing you choose should be baked separately, as this too will absorb the bird's juices and make the meat dry.

1 fresh turkey, weighing 12 to 14 pounds
1 tablespoon Bell's Poultry Seasoning
   Freshly ground black pepper (20 turns of the mill)
1 lemon
3 cloves garlic, crushed
1 stick (½ cup) sweet butter
2 cups medium-dry sherry

BEURRE MANIÉ
1 tablespoon water chestnut powder
1 tablespoon sweet butter, at room temperature

1 cup Chicken Stock (see pp. 76–77) or turkey stock

1. Bring a large kettle of water to a rolling boil. Remove the giblets from the cavity of the turkey. Rinse the bird inside and out under cold running water. Hold the turkey by its wings and allow to drain. Place the turkey in the sink and pour the kettle of boiling water over the outside of the bird, reaching all parts of the skin. You should see the skin tighten up. If the temperature is between 35 and 45 degrees and it is a clear, windy day, air-dry the turkey outside for 1 day or place the turkey breast-side down on a rack in a large shallow roasting pan and allow it to air-dry in the refrigera-

tor uncovered for 24 to 36 hours. After the first 12 hours, turn the turkey breast-side up.

2. About 4 hours before roasting the turkey, season it inside and out with the poultry seasoning and pepper. Cut the lemon in half, then squeeze the juice directly into the cavity. Place the lemon halves, along with the garlic cloves and butter, inside the cavity of the bird.

3. Preheat the oven to 350°. Adjust the level of the oven rack to the lower third so that the turkey will clear the ceiling of the oven. Place the turkey breast-side down on a rack resting in a shallow roasting pan. Roast for 1½ hours, checking after the first hour to see that the pan juices are not burning. After 1 to 1½ hours the pan juices should be dark brown. Then start adding the sherry, up to 2 cups during the whole roasting procedure. If you need more liquid, add water or turkey stock after that. Remove the roasting pan with the bird from the oven; turn the turkey breast-side up; then return the roasting pan to the oven, continuing to roast the turkey for another 1½ to 2 hours. Turn the oven down to 325° if the turkey is browning too quickly. The total roasting time will be about 3 to 3½ hours. *Do not baste the bird the entire time it is roasting.* At the end of the cooking period, the turkey should be golden brown and crisp. Remove the turkey and the roasting pan from the oven. Place the turkey, still on the rack, on a wooden carving board.

4. Prepare the beurre manié by kneading the water chestnut powder with the softened butter. Knead with the heel of your hand until it has been well combined.

5. To prepare a natural sauce: Pour the liquid from the roasting pan into a fat separator or a 4-cup Pyrex measuring cup. Defat, then return the liquid to the roasting pan, along with the chicken or turkey stock. Stirring with a wooden spoon, simmer the coagulated juices over direct heat until they are incorporated into the sauce. Add the beurre manié to the simmering sauce, stirring well until the sauce has thickened. While the turkey has been resting on the rack on the carving board, juices will have accumulated. Add these juices to the thickened sauce. Turn off the

heat and pour the sauce into a serving bowl. The turkey should be allowed to rest at least 15 to 20 minutes before carving.

My favorite method for air-drying the turkey skin before roasting is first to pray for cold, dry, sunny, humidity-free days before and on Thanksgiving day, then to put the turkey on my terrace for 24 to 48 hours, turning the bird breast-side up, breast-side down, alternately every 12 hours. The skin actually feels so taut and dry it is almost crisp before it is roasted.

You can make a quick turkey stock by simmering the turkey neck, gizzard, heart, black peppercorns, and a few leek greens in water to cover for 2 hours while the turkey is roasting.

SERVES 10 to 12

Deep-fried Marinated Quail

This recipe requires advance planning because of the long marinating time but the preparation and cooking time is minimal.

MARINADE
1 tablespoon hoisin sauce
1 tablespoon dark soy sauce
1 tablespoon medium-dry sherry
1 clove garlic, crushed

6 small quails, rinsed and drained

4 cups peanut oil for deep-frying

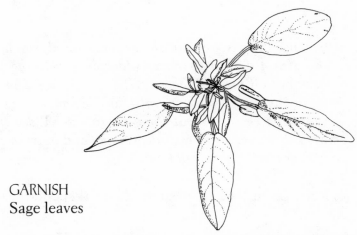

GARNISH
Sage leaves

1. Make the marinade in a medium-size bowl by mixing together the hoisin sauce, soy sauce, sherry, and garlic. Stir until well combined. Dry the quails well with paper towels inside and out. Place the quails in the bowl and massage them inside and out with the marinade. Place the bowl in the refrigerator and allow the quails to marinate at least 6 hours or overnight.

2. Remove the quails from the refrigerator 30 minutes before frying.

3. Place a wok over a high heat for about 1 minute or until it smokes. Add the peanut oil and heat until it reaches 350°. Lower the quails 3 at a time into the hot oil and deep-fry for 5 minutes at 325°. Using long cooking chopsticks, turn them once at midpoint. Remove the quails from the wok with a wire strainer and drain well on paper towels. Reheat the oil to 350°, then lower the remaining 3 quails into the oil and deep-fry for 5 minutes at 325°. Turn once. Remove them from the wok, then drain on paper towels. Allow them to cool for 5 minutes. Quarter the quails and garnish with sage leaves. Serve immediately.

SERVES 3

Braised Rock Cornish Hens
in Oyster Sauce

Because these Rock Cornish hens are braised, you may cook the dish a day in advance, which is a welcome piece of information for most cooks. When preparing them ahead, do not reduce the sauce until just before serving. To re-warm the hens, preheat the oven to 350°. Place the hens with the sauce in a covered casserole and heat for 10 minutes or until they are hot within.

2 Rock Cornish hens, weighing 1¼ to 1½ pounds each

MARINADE
12 whole shallots
4 cloves garlic, crushed
5 thin slices ginger
2 tablespoons dark soy sauce
2 tablespoons oyster sauce
Freshly ground black pepper (15 turns of the mill)
¼ cup medium-dry sherry
1 tablespoon Oriental sesame oil
2 teaspoons sugar

2 tablespoons peanut oil
¼ cup Chicken Stock, preferably salt-free (see pp. 76–77)

1. Rinse the Rock Cornish hens, then pat them dry with paper towels.

2. To make the shallots easier to peel, place them in a strainer and pour boiling water over them. Peel the shallots and leave them whole.

3. In a bowl large enough to hold the hens and the marinade, mix together the shallots, garlic, ginger, soy sauce, oyster

sauce, pepper, sherry, sesame oil, and sugar. Add the hens and coat them well. Marinate for 2 hours.

4. Place a 3- to 4-quart heat-proof casserole over high heat. Add the peanut oil and heat until hot. Remove the hens from the marinade and place them breast-side down in the casserole. Turn the heat to medium and cover. Brown for 3 minutes. Remove the cover and turn the hens over. Cover again and cook for another 3 minutes.

5. Add the marinade and the chicken stock. Cover again and simmer the hens over medium-low heat for 30 minutes, turning them over once after 15 minutes. Remove the hens from the casserole and place them on a heated serving dish.

6. Remove the sauce from the casserole and defat in a fat separator. Return the sauce to the casserole and boil it down to a thick, syrupy glaze.

7. While the sauce is reducing, cut the hens into serving pieces with poultry shears. Pour the sauce over the hens and serve immediately.

SERVES 2 to 4

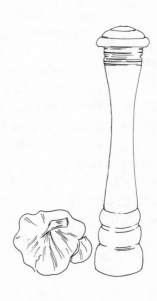

Sherry Mustard Roasted Rock Cornish Hens

Placing Rock Cornish hens on this Chinese version of a mirepoix (mixture of chopped vegetables) enhances their flavor. The secret to the sauce is to allow the pan drippings to turn dark brown before adding the veal stock. This may happen anytime after the first 30 minutes of cooking.

4 whole Rock Cornish hens, weighing 1¼ to 1½ pounds each
4 teaspoons Sichuan Peppercorn Powder (see page 13)
2 teaspoons salt
2 tablespoons sweet butter
2 cups chopped Spanish onion
1 cup diced carrot
2 cups diced bok choy, white and green parts included
1 cup Veal Stock (see page 77)
½ cup medium-dry sherry
2 teaspoons Spicy Mustard Sauce (see page 14)
2 tablespoons heavy cream

1. Preheat the oven to 450°.
2. Rinse, then drain the Rock Cornish hens. Dry them very well. Rub the hens with Sichuan Peppercorn Powder and salt.
3. Melt the butter in a small skillet. Set aside.
4. Place the onions, carrots, and bok choy in the center of a shallow roasting pan. Place the hens breast-side up on the bed of vegetables, leaving a small space between each hen. Dribble ½ tablespoon of melted butter over each breast. Roast them in the oven for 10 minutes at 450°, then reduce the heat to 400° and continue to roast for another 40 minutes. Check from time to time to see that the juices on the bottom of the roasting pan are not starting to burn. If they are very dark brown and crusty, add ½ cup of the veal stock.

5. After the 50-minute roasting period, remove the hens from the oven. Insert chopsticks or a wooden spoon into the cavity of the hens, tilt them over the roasting pan and allow the juices to drain back into the pan. Transfer the hens to a platter.

6. Place the roasting pan over medium heat. Add the veal stock and the sherry; reduce by half. While deglazing, continuously stir the veal stock and sherry in the saucepan so as to incorporate all the coagulated juices into the sauce. Add the Spicy Mustard Sauce and continue to stir another minute or until the sauce has thickened. Pour in the cream. Turn the heat to low, continuing to stir another few seconds.

7. Quarter or halve the Rock Cornish hens. Place them on a serving platter. Spoon the sauce onto the platter around (not on) the birds.

If you don't have veal stock on hand, you can substitute any kind of poultry stock.

If you want to make only 2 Rock Cornish hens, decrease all the ingredients by half with the exception of the stock and the sherry, which you will need in full. The drippings will turn brown sooner so don't allow them to burn, otherwise the sauce will have a burnt flavor as opposed to the spectacular one intended.

SERVES 6 to 8

Eight Jewel Roasted
Rock Cornish Hens

This festive way of preparing Rock Cornish hens elevates a common bird to a new category. The stuffing is so good, I frequently bake it in a covered casserole on Thanksgiving to go with my Peking Turkey. It is a delicious accompaniment to any type of roasted poultry.

The idea for this recipe originated with the classic Cantonese Eight Jewel Duck, a dish calling for the boning of a duck. But not many people want to take the time to bone a duck, so besides changing the stuffing from sweet rice to wild rice, I am now using Rock Cornish hens instead of duck. The hens contain so little fat that they do not need to be boned, whereas if you didn't bone the duck, it would be too greasy.

4 Rock Cornish hens with the giblets (including the liver, gizzard, and heart), weighing approximately 1¼ pounds each
¼ cup dried Chinese mushrooms
1 tablespoon reduced mushroom stock (see step 2)
2 cups Chicken Stock, preferably salt-free (see pp. 76–77)
¾ cup raw wild rice
⅓ cup fresh chestnuts
¼ cup diced Westphalian ham
2 whole scallions, cut into ⅛-inch rounds
1 tablespoon dark soy sauce
1 tablespoon oyster sauce
3 tablespoons sweet butter
1 teaspoon salt
⅔ cup dry white wine

SPECIAL EQUIPMENT
4 poultry skewers

1. Rinse the hens under cold running water, then pat dry with paper towels. Dice the giblets.

2. Rinse the mushrooms under cold running water. In a small bowl, soak them in cold water to cover for about 1 hour or until soft. Squeeze them over the bowl. Remove the stems and dice the mushrooms. Set the mushrooms aside. Place the stems in a small saucepan. Add the mushroom liquid. Reduce until about 1 tablespoon remains. Strain the mushroom stock, then add it to the chicken stock. Discard the stems.

3. Rinse the rice, then drain. In a 1-quart saucepan with a tight-fitting cover, bring the rice and the chicken-mushroom stock to a rapid boil over high heat. Stir with chopsticks. Turn the heat to low. Cover and simmer 45 minutes to 1 hour or until the stock has evaporated. Allow the rice to relax another 30 minutes.

4. Using a cleaver make crisscross cuts in each chestnut. Parboil them for 5 minutes, then peel and dice small.

5. Add the chestnuts, giblets, mushrooms, ham, scallions, soy sauce, and oyster sauce to the rice. Mix well.

6. Preheat the oven to 400°.

7. Place equal amounts of the stuffing into the cavity of each Rock Cornish hen. To prevent the stuffing from falling out, fasten the tail end opening of each hen with a poultry skewer. Melt the butter and spoon it evenly over the hens.

8. Place the hens breast-side up in a shallow roasting pan with no rack. The pan should be big enough so that the birds have at least 1 inch of space between them otherwise they will not brown properly. Roast the hens for 50 minutes. During the last 20 minutes sprinkle the hens with the salt and pour ⅓ cup of the wine into the bottom of the roasting pan to prevent the drippings from burning. Remove the hens from the oven and transfer them to a flat serving dish.

9. Pour off all the juices from the roasting pan into a Pyrex measuring cup, then into a fat separator; remove the fat. Pour the defatted juices back into the roasting pan. Add the remaining ⅓ cup wine and reduce the sauce, stirring occasionally, until a natural glaze is formed. Pour the sauce on top of the hens and serve immediately.

(continued)

The secrets to cooking Rock Cornish hens are to roast them without a rack, since they do not have a lot of fat; not to overcook them because the meat will become dry; and not to baste them, as that will prevent the skin from becoming crisp.

The chestnuts called for in this recipe are American chestnuts, not Chinese water chestnuts.

For the Westphalian ham you can substitute either a good country smoked ham or baked Virginia ham.

You can use jarred peeled chestnuts as a substitute; they don't need peeling or parboiling.

This recipe can be prepared early in the day through step 5.

SERVES 4

Orange Spiced Duck

The French have an expression that comes to mind when I make this dish: "La sauce est toute!" meaning the sauce is everything. In this recipe for braised duck, this memorable sauce achieves its intense flavor through the lazy long simmering, the eventual reduction to a thick syrupy glaze, and the permeating seasonings of leeks, orange, and five spice powder. I suggest a plain rice accompaniment to soak up the sauce.

    I first learned this dish from Madame Grace Zia Chu in 1967. She is the woman with whom I originally studied Chinese cooking and to whom I owe a great deal.

1 fresh Long Island Duck, weighing about 5 pounds
2 cups salt-free duck stock (see step 1) or Chicken Stock
    (see pp. 76–77)
2 fresh navel oranges
1 piece fresh orange zest (see step 3)
1 medium-size leek
¼ cup dark soy sauce
½ cup medium-dry sherry
2 tablespoons honey
1 teaspoon five spice powder
1 piece dried orange peel, 1 inch by 2 inches
1 tablespoon orange flavored liqueur

    1. Remove the neck and giblets from the duck. Place them in 1 quart of water and simmer for 1 hour or until 2 cups remain. Strain the duck stock before using. Alternatively, a chicken or general poultry stock can be substituted. In either case, they must be salt-free because of the large amount of soy sauce used in the recipe.

    2. Remove the pockets of fat from the cavity of the duck. Cut off the skin extending from the neck, leaving approximately 3

inches. Lift the skin on the neck side and remove the excess fat, glands, and membranes. Rinse the duck under cold running water; drain, then wipe dry.

3. Peel the oranges. Cut them in half, then cut each half into slices. Set aside 1 large piece of orange zest, approximately 1 inch by 3 inches.

4. Preheat the oven to 400°. Place the duck on a rack in a roasting pan, and roast it in the oven for 1 hour. To help drain the fat, prick the duck with a trussing needle along the back and also between the thighs and legs. Do this after the first 30 minutes, then again after 45 minutes. Remove the duck from the oven (the rest of the cooking is done on top of the range).

5. Remove the root end of the leek, then split the leek in half lengthwise all the way through. Place it under forcefully running warm water to remove all traces of sand. Then cut the leek into 2-inch pieces. The yield should be 2 cups cut leeks.

6. Distribute the leeks on the bottom of a wok. Insert a wooden spoon into the cavity of the duck; carefully transfer it from the roasting pan to the wok, keeping it level so as not to lose the juices that have accumulated during the roasting period. Place the duck on top of the leeks, breast-side up. Pour out the fat from the roasting pan.

7. Deglaze the roasting pan by pouring the duck stock into the pan and, with the heat on high, stirring with a wooden spoon so as to incorporate all the coagulated juices into the stock.

8. Turn the heat to high under the duck. Add the soy sauce and sherry directly over the duck. Bring to a boil.

9. Add the duck stock from the roasting pan around the sides of the wok and bring to a boil again. Cover, turn the heat to low, and simmer for 30 minutes.

10. Dribble the honey directly over the duck. Add the five spice powder, dried orange peel, and fresh orange zest to the sauce. Stir until the five spice powder has dissolved. Baste the duck a few times. Continue to cook, covered, for 1½ hours or until the duck is very tender. Set the timer every 20 minutes to baste the duck and to check that the juices do not evaporate.

11. Slip a spatula underneath the rack and remove the duck. Place it on a large, flat, heated serving platter.

12. Using a fat separator, defat the sauce.

13. If the sauce is thin, reduce it by placing the wok over high heat and stirring until it is a thick, syrupy glaze. The yield should be about ⅔ cup. Turn off the heat and add the liqueur.

14. Pour the sauce over the duck, and place the orange slices over and around it. Carve the duck by inserting 2 pairs of chopsticks into the breast and then pulling the chopsticks in opposite directions. The meat will then fall off the bones. Serve immediately.

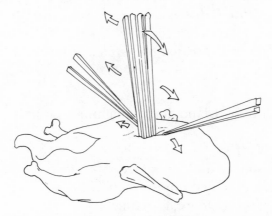

Dried orange peel is purchased in plastic bags in Chinese markets. Stored in a glass jar, it will last indefinitely. It is said to improve with age like a good Bordeaux.

Five spice powder is composed of 5 different spices: fennel, anise, cinnamon, clove, and Sichuan peppercorns. It is purchased in plastic bags and then stored in a glass jar, preferably in the refrigerator, which will preserve its aroma.

You can make Orange Spiced Duck a day in advance and rewarm it in the oven or on top of the stove. The skin is not eaten as it is not crisp; however, because the duck is braised, there will be three delicious parts to this dish: the meat of the duck, the sauce, and the leeks.

SERVES 4

Barbecued Roast Duck

*Ten years ago I sat through a 15-course banquet in China-
town. There was one disappointing dish after the next,
with one exception: Barbecued Roast Duck. I adapted this
dish. You won't have a better roast duck anywhere in the
world after you eat this one. Moist meat, crisp skin, deli-
cately seasoned. You can serve it hot with a sauce made of
the natural drippings, or room temperature as a duck
salad. Even after the duck cools off, the skin will still
remain crisp because of the blanching and air-drying technique.*

1 fresh Long Island duck, weighing 5 pounds

MARINADE
2 tablespoons dark soy sauce
1 tablespoon medium-dry sherry
1 tablespoon Oriental sesame oil
2 teaspoons minced garlic
1 teaspoon five spice powder

2 thin slices ginger
2 whole scallions, cut into 2-inch pieces
¼ cup medium-dry sherry
½ cup Chicken Stock (see pp. 76–77)

BINDER
2 teaspoons water chestnut powder
1 teaspoon medium-dry sherry

Special Equipment
Butchers' twine

1. Bring a large pot of water to a rolling boil.
2. *To Prepare the Duck:* Remove the pockets of fat lodged

inside the cavity. Also remove the giblets. Using your fingers, make a hole to remove the fat lodged between the thigh and the leg on the interior of both sides of the duck. Working with the duck breast-side up, lift the piece of skin that extends over the neck and remove the excess fat, glands, and membranes with a sharp flexible boning knife. Do not cut off this piece of skin, because when the duck is roasted the skin shrinks, and this piece is needed to cover the breast. Beginning at the neck end of the cavity, with the bird still lying breast-side up, carefully separate the skin from the meat, going down about 5 inches, by pulling the skin back with one hand and cutting with a boning knife through the fat and membranes with the other hand. Turn the duck breast-side down and do the same procedure along the top part of the back, separating the skin from the meat for about 2 inches. Turn the duck breast-side up. Put your hand underneath the outside of the skin and, with the boning knife, carefully shave off more excess fat from the inside of the skin. Do not make a hole in the skin.

3. Place the duck in the sink. Pour the boiling water over the outside of the duck on all its sides. You will see the skin tighten.

4. Loop butchers' twine around the wings if you are hanging the duck outside or inside.

5. *To Air-Dry the Duck, Method 1, Outside*: If the temperature is between 35° and 45° and it is a clear, windy day, hang the duck outside for 8 to 24 hours or until the skin is dry and taut.

Method 2, Inside: Air-dry the duck with a portable electric fan for 4 hours, 2 hours on the breast side, 2 hours on the back side. Another possibility is to air-dry it in the refrigerator by placing the duck on a rack resting on a plate and changing the position of the duck, breast-side up, breast-side down, every 12 hours. The duck's skin should be dry after 24 hours.

6. When the duck skin is dry, make the marinade by mixing together the soy sauce, the 1 tablespoon sherry, the sesame oil, garlic, and five spice powder. Stir until well combined.

7. Preheat the oven to 350°.

8. Massage the duck with the marinade for several minutes inside and out.

9. Place the ginger and scallions in the cavity of the duck.

10. *To Roast the Duck*: Remove the butchers' twine from the

duck. Place the duck breast-side up on a high-legged rack resting in a shallow roasting pan. Place the pan on the middle rack of the oven and roast the duck for 50 minutes. After about 30 minutes, add 2 cups of water to the bottom of the roasting pan to prevent the juices from burning.

11. At the end of the 50-minute roasting time, remove the roasting pan with the duck from the oven. Insert a wooden spoon in the cavity and tilt the duck, tail-end down, over a 4-cup Pyrex measuring cup. Empty all the fat and juices into the cup. Also pour in the fat and juices from the bottom of the roasting pan.

12. Place the duck breast-side down on the rack in the roasting pan. Roast another 50 minutes, still at 350°. Add water from time to time to prevent the juices from burning.

13. Remove the roasting pan with the duck from the oven. Again insert a wooden spoon into the cavity and tip the duck's fat and juices into the measuring cup. Also pour in the fat and juices from the bottom of the roasting pan.

14. Turn the duck over again and raise the oven temperature to 450°. Roast the duck breast-side up for 10 to 15 minutes at 450°. Add more water to the bottom of the roasting pan when needed.

15. Remove the duck from the oven and allow it to cool on the rack for 5 minutes.

16. Pour the contents of the roasting pan, including the fat, water, and juices, into the measuring cup. Remove the fat with a fat separator. Pour the defatted liquid back in the roasting pan along with the accumulated defatted juices. Add the ¼ cup sherry and the chicken stock to the roasting pan. Turn the heat to high and reduce the liquid in the roasting pan to ½ cup.

17. While the liquid is reducing, make the binder by dissolving the water chestnut powder in the 1 tablespoon sherry. Stir until well combined.

18. Add the binder gradually to the sauce until it thickens, about 2 minutes. Turn off the heat.

19. There are two ways of serving the duck. Western-style would be to quarter it. The traditional Chinese way would be as follows: Using a heavy cleaver and rubber mallet, chop the duck through the skin and bones into bite-size pieces. Reshape the

pieces on a serving platter to resemble the whole bird flattened out. Serve the sauce separately.

The sauce for this duck is so good, your guests will beg for more but there will be none. Reduction leads to intensity.

SERVES 3 to 4

Sichuan Peppercorn Roast Duck

Classic Sichuan Roast Duck is first marinated, steamed, and then deep-fried. That's the way the Chinese sometimes achieve a crisp skin on a duck, since most homes do not have ovens. Frying a duck, however, can be quite cumbersome, so I adapted the recipe for roasting.

Besides changing the cooking technique of the traditional dish, I also changed the seasonings. Blending Sichuan Peppercorn Powder, ginger, and scallion with fresh rosemary, candied orange peel, and marmalade gives this roast duck a delicious original taste.

1 fresh Long Island duck, weighing 5 pounds
1 tablespoon Sichuan Peppercorn Powder (see page 13)
½ lemon
2 thin slices ginger
1 whole scallion
1 branch fresh rosemary
1 garlic clove, crushed
1 teaspoon salt

BINDER
1 teaspoon water chestnut powder
1 tablespoon medium-dry sherry

⅓ cup medium-dry sherry
¼ cup Chicken Stock, preferably salt-free (see pp. 76–77)
2 tablespoons minced candied orange peel
1 tablespoon English orange marmalade

Special Equipment
Butchers' twine

1. Bring a large pot of water to a rolling boil.

2. *To Prepare the Duck:* Remove the pockets of fat lodged inside the cavity. Also remove the giblets. Using your fingers, make a hole to remove the fat lodged between the thigh and the leg on the interior of both sides of the duck. Working with the duck breast-side up, lift the piece of skin that extends over the neck and remove the excess fat, glands, and membranes with a sharp flexible boning knife. Do not cut off this piece of skin, because when the duck is roasted the skin shrinks, and this piece is needed to cover the breast. Beginning at the neck end of the cavity, with the bird still lying breast-side up, carefully separate the skin from the meat, going down about 5 inches, by pulling the skin back with one hand and cutting with a boning knife through the fat and membranes with the other hand. Turn the duck breast-side down and do the same procedure along the top part of the back, separating the skin from the meat for about 2 inches. Turn the duck breast-side up. Put your hand underneath the outside of the skin and, with the boning knife, carefully shave off more excess fat from the inside of the skin. Do not make a hole in the skin.

3. Place the duck in the sink. Pour boiling water over the outside of the duck on all its sides. You will see the skin tighten. Rub the duck inside and out with the Sichuan Peppercorn Powder.

4. Loop butchers' twine around the wings if you are hanging the duck outside or inside.

5. *To Air-dry The Duck, Method 1, Outside:* If the temperature is between 35° and 45° and it is a clear, windy day, hang the duck outside for 8 to 24 hours or until the skin is dry and taut.

Method 2, Inside: Air-dry the duck with a portable electric fan for 4 hours, 2 hours on the breast side, 2 hours on the back side. Another possibility is to air-dry it in the refrigerator by placing the duck on a rack resting on a plate and changing the position of the duck, breast-side up, breast-side down, every 12 hours. The duck's skin should be dry after 24 hours.

6. When ready to roast the duck, preheat the oven to 350°.

7. Remove the butchers' twine from the wings. Squeeze the juice of the lemon directly into the cavity. Place the lemon, ginger, scallion, rosemary branch, and garlic clove inside the cavity.

8. *To Roast the Duck:* Place the duck breast-side up on a high-legged rack resting in a shallow roasting pan. Place the pan on the middle rack of the oven and roast the duck for 50 minutes. After about 30 minutes, add 2 cups of water to the bottom of the roasting pan to prevent the juices from burning.

9. At the end of the 50-minute roasting time, remove the roasting pan with the duck from the oven. Insert a wooden spoon into the cavity and tilt the duck, tail-end down, over a 4-cup Pyrex measuring cup. Empty all the fat and juices into the cup. Also pour in the fat and juices from the bottom of the roasting pan.

10. Turn the duck over and sprinkle ½ teaspoon salt along the back. Place the duck breast-side down on the rack in the roasting pan. Roast for another 50 minutes, still at 350°. Add water from time to time to prevent the juices from burning.

11. Remove the roasting pan with the duck from the oven. Again insert a wooden spoon into the cavity and tip the duck's fat and juices into the measuring cup. Also pour in the fat and juices from the bottom of the roasting pan.

12. Turn the duck over again and raise the oven temperature to 450°. Sprinkle the remaining ½ teaspoon salt along the breast side. Roast the duck breast-side up for 10 to 15 minutes at 450°. Add more water to the bottom of the roasting pan when needed.

13. Remove the duck from the oven and allow it to cool on the rack for 5 minutes.

14. Make a binder by dissolving the water chestnut powder in 1 tablespoon sherry. Mix until well combined.

15. While the duck is cooling, make the sauce. Pour the contents of the roasting pan, including the fat, water, and juices, into the measuring cup. Remove the fat with a fat separator. Pour the defatted liquid back into the roasting pan along with the accumulated defatted juices. Add the ⅓ cup sherry. Turn the heat to high and reduce the sauce, stirring occasionally, to approximately ½ cup. Add the chicken stock, orange peel, and orange marmalade. Stir until the sauce has thickened naturally. If necessary, add the binder.

16. Quarter the duck and serve it with accompanying sauce.

A much simpler version of this recipe would be to substitute chicken for the duck, in which case you could eliminate the first step, which involves defatting the duck and separating the skin from the meat.

SERVES 4

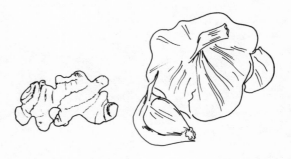

Beef, Veal, Pork, and Lamb

FILLET OF BEEF WITH SPICY SAUCE

SICHUAN STEAK AU POIVRE

FIVE SPICE BRAISED BRISKET

VEAL FILLET WITH SICHUAN SAUCE

VEAL CHOPS WITH SICHUAN SAUCE

SOONG STUFFED LOIN OF VEAL

VEAL CHOPS WITH BLACK MUSHROOM
MUSTARD SAUCE

SCALOPPINE WITH LEMON BLACK BEAN SAUCE

RACK OF VEAL LARDED WITH HAM
AND CHINESE MUSHROOMS

BARBECUED BONELESS RACK OF VEAL

BARBECUED ROAST LOIN OF PORK

PORK CHOPS WITH SPICY TOMATO SAUCE

BARBECUED BUTTERFLIED LEG OF LAMB

CHINESE SHISHKEBOB

HUNAN LAMB WITH SWEET PEPPERS
AND VIDALIA ONIONS

Fillet of Beef with Spicy Sauce

It sounds like heresy to throw a beautiful piece of filet mignon into boiling water, but the French have long known that a moist, tender result is achieved by cooking this cut of meat with this technique. Fillet of Beef with Spicy Sauce is a perfect choice as part of a buffet.

1 piece of filet mignon (cut from the tail end), weighing 1½ pounds after it is trimmed

SAUCE
1 teaspoon minced garlic
¼ cup chopped red sweet pepper
¼ cup chopped yellow Holland pepper
¼ cup sliced (⅛-inch rounds) scallions, white and green parts included
2 teaspoons Hot Sauce (see pp. 10–11)
3 tablespoons Oriental sesame oil
3 tablespoons light soy sauce
2 tablespoons red wine vinegar
1 tablespoon balsamic vinegar
2 tablespoons sugar

1. Bring a large pot of water to a rolling boil and add the meat. Cover and let boil for 15 minutes over high heat. Remove the meat from the pot and let it drain on a rack resting on a plate. Reserve the water as a base for stock. Refrigerate the meat until it is cold. This step may be completed a day in advance.

2. Make sauce by mixing together garlic, red and yellow peppers, scallions, Hot Sauce, sesame oil, soy sauce, red wine vinegar, balsamic vinegar, and sugar. Stir until well combined.

3. One hour before serving, slice the meat thinly and arrange it in overlapping slices on a flat platter. It should be very rare. Spoon the sauce over the meat. Baste before serving.

You can do all the preparations early in the day and assemble the entire dish an hour before the doorbell rings.

SERVES 3 to 4

Sichuan Steak au Poivre

The natural crust created on this thick filet mignon, which is first marinated in a combination of Sichuan and green peppercorns and then exposed to a high sautéing temperature, is incredible. By deglazing the pan juices with cognac and a Chinese seasoning sauce, this French classic has been elevated to a new class.

1 tablespoon Sichuan Peppercorn Powder (see page 13)
1 tablespoon green peppercorns, crushed
1½ pounds filet mignon tails, trimmed weight (1 or 2 pieces)

SEASONING SAUCE
¾ tablespoon dark miso
½ tablespoon dark soy sauce
½ tablespoon hoisin sauce
2 tablespoons medium-dry sherry
1 teaspoon balsamic vinegar

2 tablespoons peanut oil
1 tablespoon sweet butter
3 tablespoons minced shallots
2 teaspoons minced garlic
2 teaspoons minced ginger
¼ cup cognac
1 tablespoon heavy cream

1. Rub the Sichuan Peppercorn Powder and the crushed green peppercorns on both sides of the filet. Allow to marinate 1 hour.

2. Make the seasoning sauce by mixing together the miso, soy sauce, hoisin sauce, sherry, and vinegar. Stir until well combined.

3. Preheat the oven to 350°.

4. Place a wok over high heat for about 1 minute or until it

smokes. Add the peanut oil and heat for a few seconds. Add the steak and sauté 5 to 6 minutes. Turn the steak over and sauté another 5 to 6 minutes. Keep the heat on high unless the steak begins to burn. The heat must be high in order to achieve a crusty exterior. Turn off the heat. Remove the steak from the wok.

5. Place the steak in a heat-proof platter. Roast uncovered for another 10 minutes in the preheated oven.

6. Pour off all the oil from the wok. Place the wok over low heat. Add the butter and heat until melted. Add the shallots; sauté for 3 minutes over low heat. Turn the heat to high. Add the garlic and ginger; stir-fry 1 minute.

7. Restir the seasoning sauce and add it to the wok all at once, stirring for about 30 seconds. Add the cognac and continue to stir; reduce for another 1½ minutes. Turn off the heat. Add the cream and stir briefly.

8. Slice the steak on a cutting board. Place the steak slices on a serving dish in an overlapping pattern.

9. Pour the juices from the steak back into the wok containing the sauce. Turn the heat to low and bring the sauce to a simmer; reduce another minute. Pour the sauce over the sliced steak. Serve immediately.

This is an entrée dish but you can also serve it as an appetizer by placing the sauce in a little dish and then the meat in overlapping slices on the platter. If you are serving it this way, choose filet mignon tails that are small, which means at least 3 tails or more to make up 1½ pounds. A bigger piece would make rounds that would not be manageable served as an appetizer. You want the size of a silver dollar or a little bigger.

Any juices that have accumulated after the steak has been removed from the oven should be added to the final sauce.

This recipe can be prepared in advance through step 4.

SERVES 4

Five Spice Braised Brisket

Maybe it's my Jewish background, but I never did get over my passion for brisket. This recipe is delicious, simple, and extremely popular with students, family, and friends.

1 small leek
1 lean brisket of beef (first cut), weighing 2½ pounds
1 tablespoon flour
4 tablespoons peanut oil
2 cloves garlic, crushed
4 thin slices ginger
2 tablespoons hoisin sauce
2 tablespoons dark soy sauce
½ cup medium-dry vermouth
½ cup Chicken Stock, preferably salt-free (see pp. 76–77)
½ teaspoon five spice powder

1. Remove the root end of the leek, then split the leek in half lengthwise all the way through. Place it under forcefully running warm water to remove all traces of sand. Then cut the leek into 1-inch pieces. The yield should be 1 cup cut leeks.

2. Sprinkle the brisket on all sides with the flour.

3. Place a Dutch oven over high heat for about 1 minute. Add the peanut oil and heat until hot but not smoking. Add the brisket and brown well on all sides. This should take about 5 to 7 minutes. Add the garlic and ginger; let sizzle a few seconds. Add the leeks; stir until they are coated with oil.

4. Add the hoisin sauce and soy sauce directly on top of the brisket. Turn the heat to low. Pour the vermouth and the chicken stock on the side of the brisket, then add the five spice powder to the liquid. Stir until dissolved. Cover and simmer for 3 to 4 hours or until the brisket is fork tender. Check occasionally to make sure there is enough liquid.

5. Remove the brisket from the Dutch oven; place it on a serving dish.

6. Using a fat separator, defat the sauce.

7. Reduce the sauce by placing the Dutch oven over high heat and stirring until the sauce reaches the consistency of a thick, syrupy glaze. Pour the sauce over the brisket. Serve immediately.

Hoisin sauce can be stored in a lidded glass jar for 1 year in the refrigerator.

Five Spice Braised Brisket can be prepared a day in advance and rewarmed in a preheated 250° oven or on top of the stove over low heat. Do not reduce the sauce until the day you are serving it.

SERVES 4 to 5

Veal Fillet with Sichuan Sauce

When I was developing recipes for this book, in order to get ideas I only ate at restaurants that were classic French, Nouvelle French, and Nouvelle American. The idea for this recipe came from Le Relais à Mougins in Palm Beach, where I had for the first time a true veal fillet. It comes from the loin of veal and weighs only ¾ to 1 pound at the most. Fillet of veal is actually the eye part of a loin veal chop. It must be ordered from a butcher with whom you do a lot of business, as it is a scarce cut of meat. While I was eating it at Le Relais à Mougins, I thought to myself that I would love to dream up a Chinese sauce to go with it. By adding minced shallots, white wine, and a dash of cream to a classic Sichuan sauce, I developed a delicious blend of seasonings for this precious little piece of meat.

1   whole fillet loin of veal, weighing ¾ pound to 1 pound
1   tablespoon flour

SEASONING SAUCE
1   teaspoon hoisin sauce
1   teaspoon bean sauce
1   teaspoon plum sauce
1   teaspoon Chinese red vinegar
1   teaspoon dark soy sauce
½   teaspoon Hot Sauce (see pp. 10–11)
1   tablespoon dry white wine

2   tablespoons olive oil

GARNISH
½   pound assorted squash miniature vegetables

1   tablespoon sweet butter
2   tablespoons minced shallots
⅓   cup Chicken Stock, preferably salt-free (see pp. 76–77)

¼ cup dry white wine
2 tablespoons heavy cream

1. Preheat the oven to 250°.
2. Sprinkle all sides of the veal fillet with flour; then shake off the excess.
3. Make the seasoning sauce by combining the hoisin sauce, bean sauce, plum sauce, vinegar, soy sauce, Hot Sauce, and wine.
4. Place a small skillet over high heat for about 1 minute. Add the olive oil and turn the heat to medium. Add the veal fillet; sauté for 12 minutes over low heat, turning the fillet on 4 different sides.
5. While the fillet is sautéing, steam the miniature vegetables for 5 minutes.
6. Remove the veal fillet to a flat serving platter and place it in the preheated oven, uncovered.
7. Remove all but 1 tablespoon of oil from the skillet. Turn the heat to low. Add the butter and heat until melted. Add the shallots, then sauté over low heat for about 2 minutes. Add the chicken stock and wine. Turn the heat to high. Reduce for another minute, stirring occasionally. Add the seasoning sauce. Continue to stir the sauce and reduce 2 minutes over medium heat. The sauce should be a thick, syrupy glaze at this point. Add the cream to the skillet, stirring another minute over the lowest possible heat.
8. Take the veal fillet out of the oven and pour any juice that has accumulated into the skillet. Keep the heat on low under the skillet while you slice the fillet. Place it on the platter, then pour the sauce over it. Garnish with the steamed miniature vegetables.

For the miniature vegetables, you can substitute a combination of roll-oblique cut yellow squash and zucchini.

Plum sauce is a prepared Chinese condiment that can be purchased in many supermarkets and all Chinese grocery stores.

Bean sauce, not to be confused with fermented black bean sauce, is made from a base of fermented soy beans.

Hoisin, bean, and plum sauce are purchased in cans. Once they are opened, they should be stored in lidded glass jars in the refrigerator and will last 1 year.

All of the preparations can be done early in the day; however, the cooking must be done at the last minute.

SERVES 2

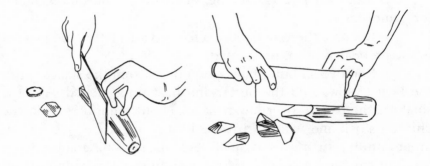

Veal Chops with Sichuan Sauce

This is a substitute recipe for Veal Fillet with Sichuan Sauce when veal fillet is not available. I have also tried this recipe with sautéed chicken breasts, split with the skin and bone, and it is equally delicious. The sautéing time of the chicken is 20 minutes.

2   veal chops, about 1-inch thick, weighing approximately
      1¼ pounds
1   tablespoon flour

SEASONING SAUCE
1   teaspoon hoisin sauce
1   teaspoon bean sauce
1   teaspoon plum sauce
1   teaspoon Chinese red vinegar
1   teaspoon dark soy sauce
½   teaspoon Hot Sauce (see pp. 10–11)
1   tablespoon dry white wine

2   tablespoons olive oil

GARNISH
½   pound assorted squash miniature vegetables

1   tablespoon sweet butter
2   tablespoons minced shallots
⅓   cup Chicken Stock, preferably salt-free (see pp. 76–77)
¼   cup dry white wine
2   tablespoons heavy cream

1. Preheat the oven to 250°.
2. Sprinkle both sides of the veal chops with flour; then shake off the excess.

3. Make the seasoning sauce by combining the hoisin sauce, bean sauce, plum sauce, vinegar, soy sauce, Hot Sauce, and wine.

4. Place a 10-inch skillet over high heat for about 1 minute. Add the olive oil, turn the heat to medium. Add the veal chops; sauté for 8 minutes over high heat, turning once at midpoint. If the veal chops are browning too fast, reduce the heat. Shake the skillet occasionally to prevent the chops from sticking.

5. While the veal chops are sautéing, steam the miniature vegetables for 5 minutes.

6. Remove the chops to a flat serving platter and place them in the preheated oven, uncovered.

7. Remove all but 1 tablespoon of oil from the skillet. Turn the heat to low. Add the butter and heat until melted. Add the shallots, then sauté over low heat for about 2 minutes. Add the chicken stock and wine. Turn the heat to high, occasionally stirring while reducing another minute. Add the seasoning sauce. Continue to stir the sauce and reduce 2 minutes over medium heat. The sauce should be a thick, syrupy glaze at this point. Add the cream to the skillet, stirring another minute over the lowest possible heat.

8. Take the veal chops out of the oven. Pour the sauce over the veal chops. Garnish with the steamed miniature vegetables.

All of the preparations can be done early in the day; however, the cooking must be done at the last minute.

For the miniature vegetables, you can substitute a combination of steamed snow peas and roll-oblique cut carrots.

SERVES 2

Soong Stuffed Loin of Veal

I had 8 students from out of town who were going to ring my doorbell at 11:00 A.M. for the first day of a week of Nouvelle Chinese cooking classes. Veal Fillet with Sichuan Sauce was on the menu and I had no fillet because my butcher was unable to acquire one. So I had to order a whole loin of veal, also known as a saddle of veal, that weighed about 5 to 6 pounds. I boned the fillet, which was surprisingly easy, then I sautéed and sauced this precious little piece of veal fillet. What to do with the leftover portion? Using a flexible boning knife, I removed the bones and was left with a boned loin roast, which I stuffed with a filling I usually use for a dish called Vegetable Package. The vegetarian stuffing is a variation of the classic Cantonese Soong dishes that usually feature chicken or lobster. "Soong" means "little pieces of meat" eaten in a lettuce package. The resulting dish is a real showpiece.

STUFFING
- ⅔ cup dried Chinese mushrooms
- 1 tablespoon reduced mushroom stock (see step 1)
- 2 tablespoons hoisin sauce
- 2 tablespoons dark soy sauce
- 2 medium-size leeks
- 2 tablespoons peanut oil
- 1 cup finely diced carrots

- One 1-inch chunk ginger
- 1 boned loin of veal, weighing 3½ pounds
- Freshly ground black pepper (10 turns of the mill)
- 4 tablespoons sweet butter, at room temperature
- 1 cup medium-dry sherry

Special Equipment
Butchers' twine

1. Rinse the mushrooms under cold running water. In a small bowl, soak the mushrooms in cold water to cover for about 1 hour or until soft. Squeeze them over the bowl. Remove the stems and dice the mushrooms. Set the mushrooms aside. Place the stems in a saucepan. Add the mushroom liquid. Reduce until about 1 tablespoon remains. Strain the mushroom stock and reserve. Discard the stems.

2. In a small bowl, combine the mushroom stock, hoisin sauce, and soy sauce. Set this seasoning sauce aside.

3. Remove the root ends of the leeks, then split the leeks in half lengthwise all the way through. Place them under forcefully running warm water to remove all traces of sand. Then finely dice the white and also the tender light green parts (reserve the dark green part for Tomato Sauce or stock). The yield should be 2 cups diced leeks.

4. Place a wok over high heat for about 1 minute or until it smokes. Add the oil and immediately after add the leeks and carrots. Turn the heat to medium and stir-fry for 3 minutes. Add the mushrooms and stir-fry another few seconds. Add the seasoning sauce. Turn off the heat. Remove the stuffing to a plate and allow to cool.

5. Preheat the oven to 450°.

6. Cut the ginger in half (peeling is not necessary), then place it in a garlic press. Open up the veal roast and extract the juice over the inside of the meat. Rub the ginger juice into the roast. Add the pepper. Evenly spread the stuffing on the veal roast. Close the roast and secure it with butchers' twine. Place the veal roast without a rack in a shallow roasting pan. Spread the butter over the top of the roast.

7. Bake for 15 minutes, then add the sherry to the bottom of the roasting pan. Turn the oven down to 350° and continue to roast for another 45 minutes. Check the roasting pan several times to see that the juices have not all evaporated. If they have, add more sherry.

8. Remove the veal from the roasting pan. Place the roasting pan over direct heat and reduce the sauce until ½ cup remains. Defatting is not necessary. Allow the veal to cool for 10 minutes before slicing.

9. Add the veal juices that have accumulated while the roast was cooling to the reduced sauce and reduce again for 1 minute. Serve the sauce separately.

The stuffing can be cooked early in the day.

SERVES 4

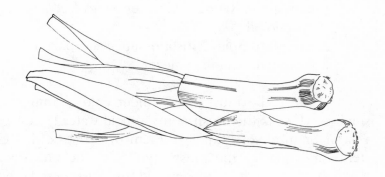

Veal Chops with Black Mushroom Mustard Sauce

This is a delicious dish that only takes 15 minutes to prepare and everyone loves it. Veal chops are expensive though, and a less costly alternative is to substitute chicken breasts. Buy 3 pounds of chicken breasts, split with the bone and the skin. Follow the recipe exactly except for the sautéing time. Chicken breasts will need 20 minutes of sautéing over medium heat. Place a loose cover over the skillet for the first 10 minutes in order to prevent excessive splattering.

½ cup dried Chinese mushrooms
1 tablespoon reduced mushroom stock (see step 1)
2 tablespoons flour
5 loin veal chops, cut 1-inch thick, weighing 3 pounds
4 tablespoons peanut oil
½ teaspoon salt
Freshly ground black pepper (20 turns of the mill)
¼ cup minced shallots
½ cup medium-dry sherry
⅓ cup Chicken Stock (see pp. 76–77)
1 tablespoon Reduced Chicken Stock (see page 78), optional
2 teaspoons Spicy Mustard Sauce (see page 14)
1 teaspoon balsamic vinegar

1. Rinse the mushrooms under cold running water. In a small bowl, soak the mushrooms in cold water to cover for about 1 hour or until soft. Squeeze them over the bowl. Remove the stems and quarter the mushrooms. Set the mushrooms aside. Place the stems in a saucepan. Add the mushroom liquid. Reduce until about 1 tablespoon remains. Strain the mushroom stock and reserve. Discard the stems.

2. Preheat the oven to 250°.

3. Sprinkle both sides of the veal chops with flour.

4. In a 14-inch skillet heat the oil until it is hot but not smoking. Add the veal chops, sprinkle them with salt and pepper. Sauté for 8 minutes over high heat, turning once at midpoint. Shake the skillet occasionally to keep the chops from sticking.

5. Turn off the heat. Transfer the chops to a flat serving platter and place them in the preheated oven, uncovered.

6. Remove all but 1 tablespoon of oil from the skillet. Add the shallots and mushrooms; sauté about 2 minutes over the lowest possible heat. Add the sherry, chicken stock, and mushroom stock. Allow to reduce. Add the Reduced Chicken Stock, Spicy Mustard Sauce, and balsamic vinegar. Continue to stir until the sauce has thickened and formed a glaze. Pour the sauce over the veal chops. Serve immediately.

All of the preparations can be done early in the day; however, the cooking must be done at the last minute.

If all the veal chops do not fit into a single skillet, sauté them in 2 skillets, in which case divide the oil and seasoning accordingly.

If you are pressed for time, soak the mushrooms in boiling water. This will soften them in 15 minutes.

I love to serve the filling for Wild Mushroom Spring Rolls as a vegetable accompaniment for these veal chops.

SERVES 5

Scaloppine with Lemon
Black Bean Sauce

This light and speedy dish features the classic Chinese Black Bean Sauce so many Americans love. It is spiked with lemon, a flavoring Italians like to use with veal.

1 pound veal scaloppine

BLACK BEAN MIXTURE
Zest of 1 lemon, grated
1½ tablespoons minced fermented black beans
1 teaspoon minced ginger
1 teaspoon minced garlic
2 whole scallions, cut into ⅛-inch rounds

BINDER
1 teaspoon water chestnut powder
2 tablespoons dry white wine
2 teaspoons dark soy sauce

¼ cup olive oil
¼ cup Chicken Stock (see page 76–77)
2 tablespoons dry white wine

GARNISH
Lemon twists (see illustration, page 169)

1. Make 1-inch slits on the outside of each piece of veal. This will prevent the veal from curling when it is sautéed.
2. Make the black bean mixture by placing the lemon zest, fermented black beans, ginger, garlic, and scallions in a bowl, then stirring until well combined.
3. Make the binder by dissolving the water chestnut powder in the wine and soy sauce. Mix until thoroughly blended.

4. Place a 12-inch skillet over high heat for about 1 minute. Add 1½ tablespoons of the olive oil and heat for a few seconds. Add one-third of the veal. Turn the heat to medium and sauté for 1 minute. Turn the pieces over and sauté 1 more minute. Transfer the scaloppine to a platter. Add another 1½ tablespoons of the olive oil and repeat the procedure with another third of the veal. Add the remaining olive oil and repeat with the last ⅓ pound of veal.

5. After all the veal has been transferred to the platter, turn the heat to low and add the black bean mixture. Stir for about 1 minute. Add the chicken stock and the 2 tablespoons wine. Stir for about 1 minute. Restir the binder and add it to the skillet, stirring until the sauce thickens. Return the scaloppine to the skillet, turning so that the pieces are glazed with the sauce. Continue to heat another few seconds. Arrange the scaloppine on a flat serving platter and garnish with lemon twists. Serve immediately.

Fermented or salted black beans are purchased in a plastic bag and will outlive us all collectively. Store them in a lidded glass jar. I like to store them in the refrigerator as that keeps them moist longer, but it is not crucial if you are short on refrigerator space.

For the veal you can substitute pork or boneless, skinless chicken breasts.

All of the preparations can be done early in the day; however, the cooking must be done at the last minute.

SERVES 3

Rack of Veal Larded with Ham and Chinese Mushrooms

This recipe was inspired by a dish I learned from Marcella Hazan, the renowned author and cooking instructor of Italian cuisine.

Frequently meat is larded with fat to make it juicier. This boneless rack of veal is larded with country smoked ham and Chinese mushrooms for flavor and aesthetics.

¼ cup dried Chinese mushrooms
1 tablespoon reduced mushroom stock (see step 1)
⅓ cup country smoked ham, cut into thin strips
1 piece of boneless rack of veal (first cut), weighing 3 pounds
12 small shallots
3 tablespoons peanut oil
4 thin slices ginger
½ cup medium-dry sherry
1 tablespoon dark soy sauce
1 tablespoon hoisin sauce

GARNISH
Watercress
Cherry tomatoes

1. Rinse the mushrooms under cold running water. In a small bowl, soak them in cold water to cover for about 1 hour or until soft. Squeeze them over the bowl. Remove the stems and cut the mushrooms into thin strips. Set the mushrooms aside. Place the stems in a saucepan. Add the mushroom liquid. Reduce until about 1 tablespoon remains. Strain the mushroom stock and reserve. Discard the stems.

2. Using a larding needle, insert alternate strips of ham and mushrooms into the veal. Lard all sides of the veal.

3. Preheat the oven to 350°.

4. To make the shallots easier to peel, place them in a strainer and pour boiling water over them. Peel the shallots and leave whole.

5. Heat the oil in an oval-shaped heavy casserole that has a tight-fitting lid. Add the veal and brown on one side about 2 minutes; turn the veal over and brown another 2 minutes.

6. Add the shallots, ginger, sherry, soy sauce, and hoisin sauce. Cover and place in the preheated oven; cook for 1 hour. While the veal is cooking, check occasionally to see that the juices have not evaporated. Add more sherry if necessary. Turn off the oven. Transfer the veal to a flat heat-proof serving platter and place inside the oven.

7. Place the casserole over medium-high heat. Stir the sauce with a wooden spoon until it becomes a thick syrupy glaze.

8. Remove the veal from the oven. Place it on a cutting board and cut it into ½-inch slices; return it to the serving platter. Pour the sauce over the veal.

9. Surround the veal with sprigs of watercress and cherry tomatoes.

You may prepare this veal dish several hours in advance and re-warm it in the oven. If preparing it in advance, do not reduce the sauce until just before serving.

Imagine a rib veal chop, then imagine a bunch of rib veal chops together, boned. This cut of meat is sometimes referred to as a boneless rib veal roast. It sounds expensive but it is about a third less than a loin veal roast, which is also known as a saddle of veal.

SERVES 4

Barbecued Boneless Rack of Veal

This marinade is a perfect blending of Eastern and Western seasonings. Marinating the veal for at least 10 hours is crucial to the taste, so plan accordingly. The boneless rack of veal is an excellent cut of veal that can be sliced into chops for sautéing or roasted whole. It is less expensive than a loin, yet every bit as tender. If your butcher does not respond to the term rack of veal, *tell him you want the part of the veal he cuts into rib chops.*

1 boneless rack of veal, weighing 2½ pounds

MARINADE
1 tablespoon dark soy sauce
2 tablespoons olive oil
1 tablespoon Spicy Mustard Sauce (see page 14)
1 tablespoon light miso
1 tablespoon medium-dry sherry
1 tablespoon minced ginger
1 teaspoon minced garlic
2 whole scallions, cut into ⅛-inch rounds
1 tablespoon green peppercorns in brine, drained and
    crushed
Freshly ground black pepper (20 turns of the mill)

1 cup veal stock (see page 77)
⅓ cup medium-dry sherry

1. Score the veal on all sides by making opposing diagonal slashes about ¼-inch deep. Place the veal in a shallow dish.
2. Make the marinade by combining the soy sauce, olive oil, Spicy Mustard Sauce, miso, and the 1 tablespoon sherry. Stir well, then add the ginger, garlic, scallions, green peppercorns, and pepper. Mix thoroughly.
3. Rub the marinade over all sides of the veal, then place the

veal in the refrigerator and allow it to marinate 8 to 10 hours. Remove the veal from the refrigerator 30 minutes before broiling.

4. Preheat the oven to broil. When the oven is very hot, place the veal on a rack resting in a shallow roasting pan. Broil the veal 3 inches from the heat source for 8 minutes. Turn the veal over. Add ½ cup of the stock to the bottom of the roasting pan and broil for another 8 minutes. Turn the oven temperature down to 350°. Remove the veal from the broiler and place it in the oven. Add the remaining ½ cup of stock and continue to roast for another 25 to 30 minutes. Check the roasting pan to see that the juices are not burning; add water if necessary. Remove the veal from the oven and place it on a wooden meat board.

5. Make a natural sauce by placing the roasting pan directly over medium-low heat and adding the ⅓ cup sherry, stirring constantly with a wooden spoon until all the drippings and the sherry have been incorporated into a sauce. Defat if necessary before serving.

6. Slice the veal into approximately ½-inch-thick pieces. Serve the sauce separately.

You can broil the veal several hours in advance.

Miso is a Japanese condiment made from a base of fermented soybeans, to which salt and another grain are added. For this recipe I prefer to use light miso to obtain the desired combination of seasonings.

Green peppercorns in brine, once opened, can be stored in the refrigerator in a glass jar for several months.

If you like your veal rare or well done, adjust the timing, as this recipe is based on veal cooked medium. I have also barbecued this veal roast on an outdoor grill with excellent results.

For the veal stock you can substitute chicken stock.

SERVES 5 to 6

Barbecued Roast Loin of Pork

Crusty on the outside, moist within, this marinated loin of pork is festive enough to serve for a holiday dinner. Accompanied by Five Spice Baked Acorn Squash and Stir-fried Watercress with Wok-Seared Tomatoes, it will provide an all-American dinner with a strong Chinese accent. Barbecued Roast Loin of Pork is definitely a recipe that a good friend of mine, Martin Naidoff, would say is "easy to prepare, but looks and tastes hard to make."

1 loin of pork, weighing 4 to 5 pounds

MARINADE
1 tablespoon minced ginger
½ cup hoisin sauce
¼ cup dark soy sauce
¼ cup American chili sauce
2 tablespoons plum sauce
2 tablespoons dark miso
⅓ cup medium-dry sherry
1 teaspoon minced garlic
3 whole scallions, cut into ⅛-inch rounds

1. Have the butcher crack the bones of the loin so that it will be easy to carve after roasting.
2. Make the marinade by mixing together the ginger, hoisin sauce, soy sauce, chili sauce, plum sauce, miso, sherry, garlic, and scallions. Rub the pork with the marinade. Place the pork with the marinade in a plastic bag, then place the bag in a bowl and allow the pork to marinate in the refrigerator for 12 hours.
3. Preheat the oven to 350°. Allow the pork to reach room temperature, remove it from the plastic bag, then place it on a rack resting in a shallow roasting pan. Roast for 1½ hours. Add some water to the bottom of the roasting pan after the first 15 minutes of roasting to prevent the juices from burning.

4. Remove the pork from the oven and allow it to cool 10 minutes. Pour off the collected juices from the roasting pan into a 4-cup Pyrex measuring cup then place them in a fat separator and remove the fat. Return the collected juices to the pan and reduce until they become a thick, syrupy glaze. Slice the roast between the bones so that each diner will have the equivalent of a single pork chop.

Don't forget to save some of the roast for the next day so that you can make a Chinese Hero or add a little leftover shredded pork to Spinach Lo Mein.

Barbecued Roast Loin of Pork may be prepared entirely in advance if you wish to serve it at room temperature.

SERVES 6

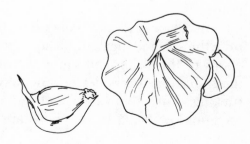

Pork Chops with Spicy Tomato Sauce

An appropriate choice for an informal family meal, this dish requires no marinating or cutting of the meat and will take just a few minutes of preparation, assuming you have on hand Hot Sauce and Tomato Sauce.

4 center loin pork chops (cut 1¼ inches thick), weighing 3 pounds

SEASONING SAUCE
½ cup Tomato Sauce (see pp. 16–17)
½ cup Chicken Stock, preferably salt-free (see pp. 76–77)
¾ cup white wine
1½ tablespoons soy sauce
1½ teaspoons Hot Sauce (see pp. 10–11)

1 to 2 tablespoons flour
¼ cup peanut oil
1 tablespoon sweet butter
1 cup chopped Spanish onion

1. Have the butcher cut the pork chops so that the bone is flat. The chops must lie flat in the skillet in order to brown properly. Make sure that each chop has a portion of the fillet.
2. Make the seasoning sauce by mixing together the Tomato Sauce, chicken stock, wine, soy sauce and Hot Sauce. Stir until well combined.
3. Lightly sprinkle the pork chops on both sides with the flour.
4. Place a 12-inch skillet over high heat for about 1 minute. Add the oil and heat until hot but not smoking. Add the pork chops to the skillet and sauté over medium-high heat for 4 minutes, shaking the skillet occasionally to prevent the chops from sticking. Turn them over and sauté for another 4 minutes over medium-low heat. If the chops are browning too fast, turn the

heat down even more. Remove the chops to a serving dish. Pour off the oil through a strainer and return the brown bits to the skillet. Add the butter, then the onions. Sauté for 2 minutes over medium heat.

5. Restir the seasoning sauce and add it to the skillet. Bring the sauce to a boil and simmer for 1 minute. Return the pork chops, along with any accumulated juices, to the skillet. Place the chops in a single layer, then baste them with the sauce. Cover and simmer for about 6 minutes, shaking the skillet occasionally. Remove the pork chops from the skillet and arrange them on a flat serving platter. Reduce the sauce another 3 minutes or until it is a thick, syrupy glaze. Pour over the chops and serve immediately.

All of the preparations can be done early in the day; however, the cooking must be done at the last minute.

SERVES 4

Barbecued Butterflied Leg of Lamb

This marinade is so flavorful and the meat is so thick that when the boned leg of lamb is run under the broiler, it develops an incredible crust that actually tastes as though you have barbecued it on an outdoor grill. The secret to obtaining a crusty exterior on meat broiled medium or rare is to choose a cut that is at least 3 inches thick so that the heat of the broiler has time to create a crust. I am sure it would be good the next day, but I have never had any left over to try.

MARINADE
1½ tablespoons light soy sauce
1½ tablespoons dark soy sauce
  2 tablespoons lemon juice
  1 tablespoon honey
  2 tablespoons hoisin sauce
  2 tablespoons Spicy Mustard Sauce (see page 14)
  3 tablespoons olive oil
  1 tablespoon Oriental sesame oil
  1 cup chopped Spanish onions
  2 teaspoons minced garlic
  2 tablespoons chopped fresh rosemary
¼ cup chopped parsley
  Freshly ground black pepper (20 turns of the mill)

½ leg of lamb (butt end), weighing 2½ pounds after boned
  and trimmed

¼ cup medium-dry sherry

1. Make the marinade by mixing together the light and dark soy sauce, lemon juice, honey, hoisin sauce, Spicy Mustard Sauce, olive oil, and sesame oil. Stir until combined, then add the onions, garlic, rosemary, parsley, and pepper. Mix until well combined.

2. Score the lamb on all sides by making opposing diagonal cuts, then massage it with the marinade. Place the lamb in a plastic bag, set it on an oval-shaped dish with a lip and refrigerate. Allow the lamb to marinate 24 to 36 hours. Bring the lamb to room temperature before broiling.

3. Heat the oven to broil for approximately 20 minutes. Remove the lamb from the plastic bag and place it on a rack resting on a shallow roasting pan. Broil for 10 to 12 minutes on each side, about 3 to 4 inches from the heat source. To prevent the drippings from burning, add the sherry to the pan after the first 12 to 14 minutes of broiling.

4. Transfer the lamb to a wooden carving board. Cool about 5 minutes. While the lamb is cooling, remove the fat from the drippings in the roasting pan. Serve this natural sauce separately. Slice the lamb. Serve immediately or at room temperature.

Serve this flavorful roast with rice and a stir-fried vegetable such as Napa Cabbage with Seared Onions and Sun-Dried Tomatoes.

SERVES 4 to 6

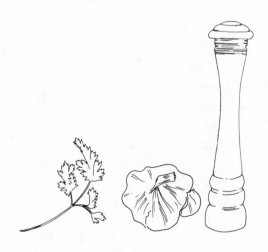

Chinese Shishkebob

In this Nouvelle Chinese version of shishkebob, the vegetables are equally as delicious as the marinated beef. In fact if you are cooking for a vegetarian, you could easily omit the meat.

MARINADE FOR THE MEAT

1½ tablespoons light soy sauce
1½ tablespoons dark soy sauce
 2 tablespoons lemon juice
 3 tablespoons olive oil
 1 tablespoon Oriental sesame oil
 1 tablespoon honey
 2 tablespoons hoisin sauce
 2 tablespoons Spicy Mustard Sauce (see page 14)
   Freshly ground black pepper (20 turns of the mill)
 1 cup chopped Spanish onion
 2 tablespoons chopped fresh rosemary
¼ cup chopped parsley
 2 teaspoons minced garlic

 3 pounds (trimmed weight) filet mignon, cubed

MARINADE FOR THE VEGETABLES

1½ tablespoons light soy sauce
1½ tablespoons dark soy sauce
 2 tablespoons lemon juice
 3 tablespoons olive oil
 1 tablespoon Oriental sesame oil
 1 tablespoon honey
 2 tablespoons hoisin sauce
 2 tablespoons Spicy Mustard Sauce (see page 14)
   Freshly ground black pepper (20 turns of the mill)

2 cups cherry tomatoes
2 cups triangle-cut sweet peppers (combination of red and
    yellow)
2 cups quartered Spanish onion

Special Equipment
Bamboo skewers

1. Make the marinade for the meat by mixing together the light and dark soy sauce, lemon juice, olive oil, sesame oil, honey, hoisin sauce, Spicy Mustard Sauce, pepper, onion, rosemary, parsley, and garlic. Stir until well combined.

2. Place the filet mignon cubes in the marinade. Mix well, then refrigerate.

3. Make the marinade for the vegetables by mixing together the light and dark soy sauce, lemon juice, olive oil, sesame oil, honey, hoisin sauce, Spicy Mustard Sauce, and pepper. Stir until well combined.

4. Place the cherry tomatoes, red and yellow peppers, and onion in the vegetable marinade. Mix well. Leave at room temperature. Allow the vegetables and refrigerated meat to marinate for 3 hours.

5. Preheat the broiler for 20 minutes. Place 4 cubes of meat on each bamboo skewer. Place the tomatoes, peppers, and onions on separate skewers, as each vegetable takes a different time to cook. Place the onions 5 inches from the heat source and broil for 15 minutes or until they are cooked all the way through. Remove them from the broiler. Place the remaining vegetables and meat as close as possible to the heat source and broil for approximately 4 to 6 minutes on each side. Serve immediately.

Chinese Shishkebob can also be grilled on an outdoor barbecue.

If you soak the bamboo skewers in water for 30 minutes, they won't burn under the broiler.

SERVES 6 to 8

Hunan Lamb with Sweet Peppers and Vidalia Onions

These Georgia onions lend a natural sweetness to this spicy, hearty dish originally from Hunan, a province in the western part of China. The traditional dish calls for scallions instead of the Vidalia onions, and raw chili peppers instead of fresh sweet peppers and Hot Sauce. Raw chili peppers are characteristic of Hunan cooking, but I prefer my homemade Hot Sauce, as the raw chili peppers make me cough and cry when I am removing the seeds and membranes. They also have a kickback when stir-fried in the wok.

1 pound boneless lamb (from the butt end of the leg)

MARINADE
1 egg white
1 tablespoon water chestnut powder
1 tablespoon medium-dry sherry

SEASONING SAUCE
2 teaspoons water chestnut powder
¼ cup medium-dry sherry
2 tablespoons dark soy sauce
1 tablespoon hoisin sauce
2 teaspoons balsamic vinegar
1 to 2 teaspoons Hot Sauce (see pp. 10–11)

1 cup peanut oil for passing through
1½ cups sliced Vidalia onions
½ cup shredded yellow Holland pepper
½ cup shredded red sweet pepper
1 teaspoon minced garlic
1 tablespoon minced ginger
1 teaspoon Oriental sesame oil

1. Cut the lamb with the grain into strips about 1½ inches wide. Partially freeze, then cut against the grain into ¼-inch slices.

2. Make the marinade by mixing together the egg white, the 1 tablespoon water chestnut powder, and 1 tablespoon sherry. Stir until well combined. Add the lamb slices to the marinade and mix well. Refrigerate for at least 1 hour or up to 12 hours.

3. Make the seasoning sauce by first dissolving the 2 teaspoons water chestnut powder in the ¼ cup sherry, then adding the soy sauce, hoisin sauce, vinegar, and Hot Sauce. Stir until well combined.

4. Place a wok over high heat for about 1 minute or until it smokes. Add the peanut oil and heat until it reaches 325°. Restir the lamb in the marinade and add half of it to the wok. Stir for about 1 minute or until the lamb loses its red color. Remove the lamb slices from the oil with a wire strainer and place them in a colander set over a bowl. Reheat the oil to 325°, or until you can no longer hear the oil splatter. If the oil is splattering too much, cover it. Add the remaining ½ pound of lamb to the oil and cook 1 minute. Pour the contents of the wok into the colander set over a bowl. Shake the colander to aid the draining, then move it to a dry bowl and shake again. Do not wash the wok.

5. Return the wok to high heat. In the oil that glazes the wok, stir-fry the onions over high heat. Allow them to scorch a little. If necessary, add a small amount of the oil in which the lamb was cooked. Add the yellow and the red peppers; stir-fry another minute. Add the garlic and ginger; stir-fry 1 minute.

6. Restir the seasoning sauce and add it to the wok all at once. Continue to stir-fry until the sauce has evenly coated the meat. Add the sesame oil. Turn off the heat. Mix briefly. Serve immediately.

For the lamb, you can substitute pork butt; boneless, skinless chicken; flank steak; or a more expensive cut of beef.

The longer the meat marinates (up to 12 hours), the more tender it becomes, so plan accordingly.

The purpose of the marinade is: The egg white makes the meat velvety, the sherry tenderizes it, and the water chestnut powder prevents the meat from absorbing oil when it is fried. If you don't have water chestnut powder on hand, you can substitute an equal amount of cornstarch.

All of the preparations can be done early in the day; however, the cooking must be done at the last minute.

SERVES 2 to 3

Desserts

KAREN LEE'S FIVE SPICE COCOA CAKE

GINGER DATE BREAD PUDDING

DATE BREAD

CANDIED GINGER CRÈME ANGLAISE

BAKED CUSTARD WITH KUMQUAT SAUCE

KUMQUAT SAUCE

ANISE PEACH COMPOTE

ALMOND BUTTER COOKIES

GINGER IN SYRUP

CARAMEL PEARS

ALMOND CREAM AMARETTI

WONTON CANNOLI

FROZEN LEMON SOUFFLÉ WITH
FRESH RASPBERRY SAUCE

FRESH RASPBERRY SAUCE

Karen Lee's Five Spice Cocoa Cake

This is a fabulous variation on applesauce cake. It is a wonderful accompaniment to Anise Peach Compote. I sometimes use the last few pieces as a substitute for the date bread in Ginger Date Bread Pudding.

Serve it topped with Candied Ginger Crème Anglaise, ice cream, or mascarpone, which is a fresh-milk cheese (sort of a cross between cream cheese and crème fraîche).

⅓ cup currants
1 tablespoon cognac
2 cups sifted all-purpose flour
1½ teaspoons baking soda
¾ teaspoon salt
    Butter for greasing
¾ cup chopped pitted dates
¾ cup chopped walnuts
½ cup sweet butter
2 tablespoons cocoa powder
½ teaspoon five spice powder
½ teaspoon cinnamon
½ teaspoon nutmeg
1½ cups sugar
2 eggs
½ cup Quatre Fruits Sauce (see page 15)
1 cup unsweetened applesauce

1. Place the currants in a small bowl. Stir in the cognac and set aside.

2. Sift the flour, baking soda, and salt together. Set the flour mixture aside.

3. Preheat the oven to 350°. Grease a Bundt pan, coating well along the bottom and sides.

4. Toss the dates and walnuts with 2 tablespoons of the flour mixture. Set the date mixture aside.

5. Place the butter, cocoa powder, five spice powder, cinnamon, and nutmeg in a large bowl. Beat at medium speed with an electric mixer. Gradually add the sugar. This procedure should take about 5 minutes.

6. Add the eggs one at a time, beating well after each addition. At low speed, beat in alternately the flour mixture, the Quatre Fruits Sauce, and the applesauce. Beat just until smooth. Stir in the date mixture, along with the currants.

7. Pour the batter into the Bundt pan and bake one hour, or until a poultry skewer that you insert into the center of the cake comes out dry.

8. Remove the cake from the oven and set it on a rack for 10 minutes to cool. Invert the Bundt pan onto another rack, then lift off the pan and allow the cake to cool thoroughly before serving.

SERVES 12

Ginger Date Bread Pudding

The idea for this luscious, comforting dessert started when a member of my family gave me a loaf of date bread. I had a few pieces then put the rest in the freezer, thinking some-day I might turn it into a bread pudding. Later, I con-sulted with Amanda Cushman, an assistant of mine for catering assignments who works in magazine test kitchens. She gave me a basic bread pudding recipe. Then, when teaching some classes in Virginia, I got the idea from my students of adding Candied Ginger Crème Anglaise. Too many cooks do not necessarily spoil the broth.

½ loaf Date Bread (see page 285)
3 tablespoons sweet butter
2 tablespoons chopped candied ginger
2½ cups milk
4 eggs, at room temperature
½ cup sugar
½ teaspoon almond extract
    Butter for greasing
1 recipe Candied Ginger Crème Anglaise (see pp. 286–287)

1. Preheat the oven to 325°.

2. Slice the Date Bread, then cut it into ½-inch cubes. The yield should be 3½ cups.

3. In a small saucepan, melt the butter. Toss the bread cubes with the melted butter and candied ginger.

4. Place the milk in a saucepan. Place over low heat until hot, stirring occasionally.

5. While the milk is heating, beat the eggs well with a wire whisk. Gradually add the sugar and almond extract to the eggs.

6. Slowly add the hot milk to the beaten-egg mixture, whisk-ing until well combined.

7. Butter a 2-quart soufflé dish. Place the bread cubes in the dish, then pour in the milk mixture. Allow to sit for 1 hour.

Place the soufflé dish in an oblong baking pan filled with hot water to a depth of 1 inch. Bake for 1 hour in the preheated oven. Serve warm or at room temperature with the Candied Ginger Crème Anglaise.

Ginger Date Bread Pudding can be baked several hours before serving.

SERVES 8

Date Bread

Although this is a delicious date bread that can be eaten plain, buttered, or with cream cheese, it is intended in this book for Ginger Date Bread Pudding. You will have enough date bread from this loaf to make two puddings plus a little for nibbling.

 1 cup diced pitted dates
1½ teaspoons baking soda
 ½ teaspoon salt
 ¾ cup boiling water
   Butter for greasing
 ¼ cup sweet butter
 ¾ cup sugar
 2 eggs
 1 teaspoon vanilla extract
1½ cups sifted flour

1. Preheat the oven to 350°.
2. In a small bowl, combine the dates, baking soda, and salt. Add the boiling water. Let stand 20 minutes.
3. Grease a 9 x 5 x 3-inch loaf pan.
4. In a medium-size bowl, cream the butter and sugar with an electric mixer. This will take about 3 minutes. Add the eggs, one at a time, beating well after each addition. Beat in the vanilla extract. On low speed, mix in the flour until just blended. Still on low speed, add the date mixture, and mix until just blended. Pour the mixture into the greased loaf pan and bake on the middle rack of the oven for 1 hour or until a poultry skewer, inserted in the center, comes out clean. Cool the Date Bread in the loaf pan for 10 minutes, then remove it to a rack to finish cooling.

Store Date Bread in the refrigerator for up to 1 week or in the freezer for up to 1 year.

YIELDS 1 loaf

Candied Ginger Crème Anglaise

Candied Ginger Crème Anglaise is wonderful with Ginger Date Bread Pudding. It is also delicious with Karen Lee's Five Spice Cocoa Cake, baked apples, poached pears, or fresh berries.

- ½ cup heavy cream
- ½ cup milk
- 1 tablespoon water chestnut powder
- 2 tablespoons cognac
- 1½ tablespoons diced candied ginger
- 2 egg yolks
- ¼ cup sugar
- 1 tablespoon sweet butter (optional), melted

1. Heat the cream and milk over low heat in a stainless steel or enamel saucepan until hot, but before a skin forms.

2. In a bowl, prepare a binder by dissolving the water chestnut powder in the cognac. Add the candied ginger and mix well.

3. In another bowl, beat the egg yolks. Gradually add the sugar, beating for several minutes or until thickened. The desired consistency is a ribbonlike flow falling from the beater when lifted over the bowl.

4. Slowly pour the heated cream-milk mixture into the egg yolk mixture, beating all the while.

5. Return this mixture to the saucepan. Turn the heat to medium-low. Stir slowly but constantly with a wooden spoon in a figure-8 motion so as to reach the center of the saucepan. Do not let the sauce rise above 170° on a candy thermometer. The sauce should be hot but not boiling; otherwise it will curdle. Heat about 2 minutes or until the mixture lightly coats the spoon; then turn the heat to low. Restir the binder and add it to the saucepan, continuing to stir in a figure-8 motion until the sauce thickens. This should take approximately another minute. Turn off the heat.

6. To prevent skin from forming, pour the crème anglaise in a bowl and cover with melted butter; or place a sheet of plastic wrap directly in contact with the crème anglaise, in which case eliminate the melted butter. Serve hot or at room temperature.

Candied Ginger Creme Anglaise can be made a day in advance and refrigerated. Allow to reach room temperature.

YIELDS approximately 1½ cups

Baked Custard with Kumquat Sauce

3½ cups milk
½ cup heavy cream
8 egg yolks, at room temperature
½ cup sugar
1 teaspoon vanilla extract
    Butter for greasing
    Kumquat Sauce (see opposite page)

1. Preheat the oven to 325°.

2. In a saucepan combine the milk and cream. Over low heat, heat the mixture until hot but not scalding, stirring occasionally with a wooden spoon in a figure-8 motion.

3. While the milk is heating, place the egg yolks in a medium-size bowl. Using a wire whisk, beat them for 1 minute. Add the sugar gradually, continuing to beat for another few minutes or until the egg yolks have lightened in color. Gradually beat in the heated milk and cream mixture, then the vanilla extract.

4. Butter 8 to 12 glass ramekins, depending on their size. Place ½ to ¾ cup custard in each ramekin. Fill a large roasting pan with boiling water to a depth of 1 inch. Place the ramekins in the roasting pan and bake for 20 minutes or until the custard has set and has browned on top. Do not overcook. To see if the custard is set, place a sharp knife in the middle; if it comes out clean, the custard is done. Remove the ramekins from the oven and place on a rack to cool.

5. Once custard is cool, place about 1 tablespoon Kumquat Sauce on top of each custard. Serve at room temperature.

YIELDS 8 to 12 custards

Kumquat Sauce

This sauce is intended for Baked Custard, however, it is a wonderful condiment to serve as you would a jam on muffins or tea breads.

1 pint kumquats
2 cups water
1 cup sugar

1. Place the kumquats in a strainer. Remove any stems and leaves. Rinse briefly under cold running water, then drain. Separate the pulp from the skins. Cut the skins into fine strips. Place the skins in a saucepan and add the water. Bring to a boil over high heat, then turn the heat to low and simmer the skins, uncovered, for about 30 minutes or until they are tender. Pour the contents of the saucepan into a strainer set over a bowl.

2. Return the liquid to the saucepan and add the sugar and the kumquat pulp. Stir until the sugar dissolves over low heat. Continue to cook over low heat for 10 minutes or until the syrup is thick. Pour the contents of the saucepan into another strainer set over a bowl. Using a wooden spoon, press down to extract as much of the syrup as possible. Discard the pulp.

3. Add the skins to the syrup, stirring to combine. Cool, then place in a lidded glass jar. Refrigerate for up to 2 months.

An alternative to making the sauce would be to melt some good-quality orange marmalade, then spoon a scant tablespoon over the top of each custard.

YIELDS approximately 1½ cups

Anise Peach Compote

This speedy and delicious dessert is best made in late summer or early fall when peaches are at their best. A slice of Karen Lee's Five Spice Cocoa Cake is a great match for this compote.

  6 medium-large peaches
  1 cup port
  3 tablespoons brown sugar
16 star anise pods or 2 whole star anise
  2 cinnamon sticks, approximately 2 inches each
    Heavy cream (optional)

1. Bring a kettle of water to a rolling boil. Submerge the peaches one at a time in the boiling water for 1 minute to loosen their skins. Remove the peaches from the water with a wire strainer and allow them to cool. Peel and slice the peaches into wedges about ⅜ inch thick.

2. In a 12-inch skillet, heat the port over medium heat for 1 minute. Add the brown sugar, star anise, and cinnamon sticks. Bring the mixture to a simmer, then turn the heat to low and stir until the sugar dissolves. Add the peaches; simmer 5 minutes or until the peaches have just cooked through. Pour the contents of the skillet into a bowl and allow the compote to cool.

3. Remove the star anise and the cinnamon sticks. Serve the peaches at room temperature, adding a teaspoon of heavy cream to each serving if desired.

The kind of port you choose should be determined by the quality you can best afford. The better the port, the better this dessert will turn out. One of my favorite ports is Porto Hutcheson, 1970.

Stored in the refrigerator, Anise Peach Compote will last for several days. Allow it to reach room temperature. Do not add the cream until just before serving.

SERVES 8

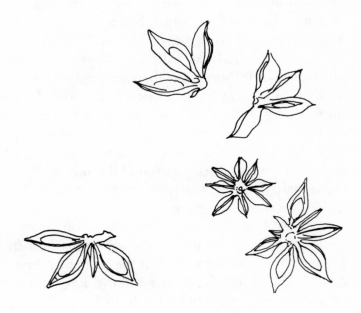

Almond Butter Cookies

These cookies are more like French butter cookies than the original Chinese almond cookies. Authentic Chinese almond cookies are made with lard instead of butter, almond flavoring instead of almonds, and yellow food coloring instead of egg yolks.

    2 cups plus 40 whole raw almonds, blanched
1½ cups flour, sifted
  ⅛ teaspoon salt
  ½ cup dark brown sugar
  ¼ cup white sugar
  ¾ cup sweet butter, cold
  2 egg yolks
  2 tablespoons almond liqueur

1. Preheat the oven to 325°. Spread all the almonds in a single layer on a cookie sheet and roast them about 15 to 20 minutes or until they are golden brown. Let the almonds cool. Reserve 40 whole almonds for garnish. Pulverize the remaining almonds in a food processor, using the on-and-off technique.

2. Place the flour, salt, and brown and white sugars in the processor bowl. Process the dry ingredients a few seconds. Cut the butter into 12 pieces, then place it in the bowl. Process the mixture until the butter has been well combined, about 10 to 12 pulses. Add the 2 cups pulverized almonds; process another few seconds. Add the egg yolks and almond liqueur; process a few more seconds. Use an icing spatula around the sides of the bowl to remove the dough. Wrap it in 2 layers of plastic wrap. Refrigerate for at least 6 hours or up to 2 days.

3. Preheat the oven to 375°. Break off tablespoon-size pieces of dough. Using the palms of your hands, roll them into balls. Flatten each ball of dough with the side of a cleaver that has been dipped into flour (this is to prevent the dough from sticking). Press until it is very thin, about ¼-inch thick.

4. Place the cookies on a cookie sheet, leaving ½ inch between each cookie. Center an almond in each cookie, pressing down firmly. Bake for 5 minutes at 375°, then reduce the oven temperature to 325° and continue to bake for another 5 to 8 minutes or until the cookies are golden brown. Remove them from the oven. With the aid of a spatula, place the cookies on a rack to cool.

Stored in a tin or a lidded glass jar, Almond Butter Cookies will keep for 1 week.

YIELDS 40 cookies

Ginger in Syrup

I love to use a sprinkling of minced Ginger in Syrup on top of Caramel Pears, baked acorn squash, baked apples, or ice cream. Once you have a batch made up in the refrigerator, you'll wonder how you ever got along without it.

½ pound ginger

SYRUP
1½ cups sugar
¾ cup cider vinegar
½ cup water
1 stick cinnamon
6 cloves
6 whole allspice
Six 4-inch strips lemon zest
½ whole nutmeg

1. Peel the ginger, then cut it into ½-inch cubes. Bring 3 cups of water to a rolling boil in a medium-size saucepan. Add the ginger. Boil 15 minutes covered, then drain. (Reserve for ginger tea if desired.)

2. To make the syrup, place the sugar, vinegar, water, cinnamon, cloves, allspice, lemon zest, and nutmeg in a 1-quart saucepan. Bring to a boil. Stir briefly, continuing to boil for 5 minutes.

3. Add the ginger to the boiling syrup. Cover and cook for 15 minutes. Remove the cover. Simmer another 5 minutes, or until the syrup is thick but still covers the ginger. Turn off the heat. Allow to cool. Place the Ginger in Syrup in a lidded glass jar. Stored in the refrigerator, it will last 1 year.

YIELDS 1½ cups

Caramel Pears

When you want fruit for dessert, Caramel Pears is a perfect choice. Bake the pears an hour or so before serving, as they are best when warm.

6 large well-ripened pears
3 tablespoons sweet butter
¾ cup loosely packed dark brown sugar
½ cup heavy cream or crème fraîche
1 tablespoon Ginger in Syrup, chopped (see opposite page)

1. Preheat the oven to 350°.
2. Stem and peel the pears. Cut them in half lengthwise, then scoop out the cores. Cut a thin slice from the side of each pear so that they will lie firmly, cored side up. Place the pears in a shallow baking dish. (Do not use Pyrex, because the last part of the recipe will require direct heat.) Evenly distribute the butter and the sugar on each pear half. Bake them for 30 minutes, basting once after 15 minutes. Transfer the pears from the baking dish to a serving platter.
3. Place the baking dish over low heat, stirring until the butter and sugar caramelizes and turns dark brown. Turn off the heat and stir in the cream, mixing well until it is blended with the caramel sauce.
4. Pour the sauce over the pears and sprinkle with the chopped Ginger in Syrup. Serve the pears hot or at room temperature.

For the pears, you can substitute apples, as they work equally well.

SERVES 6

Almond Cream Amaretti

Almond Cream Amaretti is a variation of the French crème anglaise but is lighter and less caloric as it uses a base of milk and not cream. It also has less cholesterol because of the absence of egg yolks.

1 cup raw almonds, blanched
4 cups milk
½ cup sugar
¼ cup water chestnut powder
4 tablespoons almond flavored liqueur
1 pint raspberries
6 Amaretti cookies, crushed

1. Preheat the oven to 325°.
2. Place the almonds in a shallow roasting pan and roast for about 15 minutes or until they become light brown. Remove them from the oven and allow to cool.
3. Place the roasted almonds in a food processor. Using the on-and-off technique, process until finely ground.
4. In a 2- to 3-quart saucepan, combine 3½ cups of the milk with the ground almonds and the sugar. Bring to a simmer over medium-low heat, stirring occasionally.
5. Remove the pan from the heat, cover, and let the almonds steep for 1 hour.
6. Strain the mixture through a sieve set over a bowl, pressing down hard on the almonds with the back of a wooden spoon to extract their moisture before discarding them.
7. Return the almond-flavored liquid to the saucepan and bring it to a simmer. Dissolve the water chestnut powder in the remaining ½ cup milk, stir it into the liquid, and set the pan over low heat. Stirring constantly, simmer for about 2 to 3 minutes or until the custard thickens.

8. Add half the liqueur and stir to blend.

9. Strain the custard through a sieve into a bowl. Place a sheet of plastic wrap in direct contact with the custard to prevent a skin from forming. Allow to cool at least 4 hours or overnight.

10. Two hours or more before serving, wash and dry the berries. If using strawberries, hull them but leave them whole. Toss and marinate them in the remaining 2 tablespoons of liqueur.

11. Just before serving, remove the custard from the refrigerator and beat well with a wire whisk.

12. Place the marinated berries in a glass bowl and pour the custard over them. Garnish with crushed Amaretti cookies.

Raspberries are a first choice but strawberries or blueberries will do nicely.

A trick to storing raspberries overnight is to remove them from the box immediately upon returning home and place them on a plate in a single layer. Raspberries are highly perishable, which is one of the reasons they are expensive. It is the weight of the raspberries on top of each other that causes them to release their juice, which causes mold.

When purchasing raspberries, always look them over as best you can to try to determine if there is any mold. Also look at the bottom of the box to see that it is dry with no trace of stains. This will be a good indication that they are fresh.

SERVES 6

Wonton Cannoli

My friend Rachel Sancilio, who is a fabulous cook and instructor of Italian cooking in Virginia Beach, Virginia, showed me how to use wonton skins as a substitute for making the Italian dough for cannoli, which is usually a laborious task.

FILLING
1 pound ricotta cheese
¾ cup confectioners' sugar
3 tablespoons semisweet chocolate chips (miniature size)
2 tablespoons diced candied ginger
½ teaspoon vanilla extract

2 cups peanut oil for deep-frying

12 thin square wonton wrappers

Special Equipment
6 to 12 pieces of metal tubing, 6 inches long by ½ inch in diameter
Pastry bag fitted with ½-inch pastry tube

1. Place the ricotta in a strainer set over a bowl in the refrigerator and allow to drain at least 12 hours.

2. Place the drained ricotta in a bowl along with the sugar, chocolate chips, candied ginger, and vanilla extract. Stir until the mixture is well combined, then refrigerate while frying the wonton wrappers.

3. Place a small wok (12-inch or less) over high heat for 1 minute or until it smokes. Pour in the peanut oil and heat until the oil reaches 350°.

4. While the oil is heating, prepare the cannoli shells: Lay a wonton wrapper in front of you so that it is a diamond shape. Center the metal tubing over it. Lift the wonton corner nearest

you, then wrap it loosely around the tubing. Continue to roll the wonton until it is completely wrapped around the tubing. Moisten the edge with water to seal.

5. Lower the tubings, 3 at a time, into the oil. Fry the wontons 15 to 30 seconds or until they become golden brown. Using tongs, remove one tubing at a time, carefully tilting it over the wok so that the oil drains out of the tubing back into the wok and not on you. Drain the cannoli shells on paper towels. After about 5 or 10 seconds, holding the tubing with the tongs in one hand and holding the cannoli shell with a potholder in the other, gently slip off the cannoli shell. Repeat the entire procedure until all the cannoli shells have been fried, drained, and removed from the tubing.

6. Place the cannoli filling in a pastry bag fitted with a pastry tube that is no more than ½ inch in diameter. Pipe in the filling first from one end and then from the other of each cannoli.

Cannoli shells can be made early in the day and allowed to sit at room temperature. The filling can be combined a day in advance. However, the shells should not be filled more than 30 minutes before serving.

Purchase the metal tubing at cookware shops. Another possibility is to go to a hardware store and have them cut ½-inch metal tubing into 7-inch lengths.

YIELDS 12 cannoli

Frozen Lemon Soufflé
with Fresh Raspberry Sauce

*A dessert featuring lemon has always been my favorite end-
ing to any meal. I often rely on this one. When running
short on time, I forego making the Fresh Raspberry Sauce
and instead surround the soufflé with fresh raspberries,
strawberries, or blueberries.*

1	envelope (¼ ounce) unflavored gelatin
¼	cup cold water
6	egg yolks
1	cup sugar
⅔	cup lemon juice
1	tablespoon grated lemon zest
1	tablespoon finely diced candied ginger
4	egg whites
1½	cups heavy cream
	Butter for greasing
1	recipe Fresh Raspberry Sauce (see page 302)

1. In a small bowl, dissolve the gelatin in the water.

2. Place the egg yolks in a medium-size bowl. Using a portable electric mixer, beat the yolks for about 1 minute. Gradually
add the sugar, continuing to beat until the yolks thicken and
lighten in color. Mix in the lemon juice.

3. Transfer the egg yolk mixture to a 1- to 1½-quart saucepan. Place the saucepan in a water bath. This can be done by
pouring 2 inches of water in a skillet with a lip, bringing it to a boil,
and then placing the saucepan containing the egg yolk mixture in
the water. This serves as a double boiler, also called a bain-marie.

4. Turn the heat to medium and cook this mixture until it is
slightly thickened, stirring in a figure-8 motion so as to reach the
center of the saucepan. This will take about 3 minutes. Do not
allow it to boil, because the egg yolks would curdle. Remove the

mixture from the water bath and stir in the dissolved gelatin, lemon zest, and candied ginger. Allow the mixture to cool.

5. In a medium-size bowl, beat the egg whites until they become stiff but not dry. Fold them into the cooled lemon mixture with a rubber spatula.

6. Beat the cream until it has thickened, but is not completely stiff. If the cream keeps its shape when you let it drop from the lifted beater back into the bowl, it is the proper consistency. (This is what the French call Crème Chantilly.) Using a rubber spatula, fold the cream into the lemon mixture.

7. Grease a 6-cup charlotte mold or soufflé dish. Slowly pour the lemon mixture into the mold and freeze until solid. When ready to serve, submerge seven-eighths of the mold into a bowl of hot water for approximately 5 seconds. Place a round serving platter over the exposed part of the soufflé and invert, shaking the mold a little to loosen the soufflé. It should unmold easily at that point. If not, submerge the mold for another 5 seconds.

8. Slice the soufflé into wedges. Lay each wedge on its side and spoon sauce across the center. Serve immediately.

The lemon mixture must be thoroughly cool before folding in the egg whites or whipped cream. Otherwise, the egg whites will collapse and the cream will thin out.

The soufflé can be made several days in advance and can stay in its mold in the freezer until serving.

SERVES 8 to 12

Fresh Raspberry Sauce

This colorful sauce with its intense raspberry flavor makes a refreshing, dramatic close to a special dinner when served with Frozen Lemon Soufflé or with a plain cake such as angel food or sponge cake.

2 cups water
½ cup sugar
2 pints fresh raspberries
2 tablespoons Framboise liqueur or orange flavored
    liqueur

1. Place the water and sugar in a 1-quart saucepan. Boil over medium heat for 7 to 10 minutes or until the syrup has reduced by one-half. Add the raspberries. Stir well to coat with the syrup. Continue to cook for another 5 to 10 minutes or until the raspberries have softened and the sauce is quite thick. Remove the sauce from the heat.
2. Place the sauce in a strainer set over a bowl. Using a wooden spoon, stir and press it through the strainer. Add the liqueur to the bowl and mix well. Set the sauce aside until ready to serve. Refrigerate if you are not using it within a few hours.

Fresh Raspberry Sauce can be made several days in advance.

YIELDS 1 cup sauce

Index

KAREN LEE is a nationally recognized authority on Chinese cuisine. She has supervised a highly successful catering business and cooking school since 1972. Her classes have received favorable editorial endorsements from the *New York Times*, *Bon Appetit*, *Food and Wine*, *House Beautiful*, *Better Homes and Gardens*, and *Travel and Leisure*. Her articles on food have appeared in the *New York Times Magazine*, *Food and Wine*, and *Working Woman*. She has made numerous appearances on radio and television throughout the country, and has given lecture demonstrations for retailers, cooking schools, and charitable organizations. Karen Lee has one son, Todd Hartman, who is attending college.

ALAXANDRA BRANYON, author of three off-Broadway plays, is the playwright/lyricist half of Branyon/Kitchings, a songwriting team that has written numerous pop songs and two musical comedies, the latter of which received an award from the American Society of Composers, Authors, and Publishers. As a food writer, her articles have appeared in the *New York Times Magazine*, *Food and Wine*, and *Working Woman*. She coauthored *Chinese Cooking Secrets* (Doubleday, 1983) and *Soup, Salad and Pasta Innovations* (Doubleday, 1987) with Karen Lee.